SUDDEN FAMILY

Debi and Steve Standiford
Nhi and Hy Phan

"Someone please save my brother!" cried fourteen-year-old Hy Phan. His brother, Nhi, a polio victim, had fallen overboard as they and dozens of other "boat people" fled war-ravaged Vietnam for America. Hy's cry was an echo of the wider call for help ringing out around the world from the throats of thousands of other refugees. And this is the moving story of how the love of a family motivated by the love of Christ can respond to that call.

Says Debi Standiford in her introduction to this book, "Our family has been an oasis for two boys caught in the maelstrom of war and its aftermath. Thirty years of war and a succession of totalitarian governments overcame the homeland of Nhi and Hy Phan. A way of life was destroyed. Our two sons were caught up in a chain of events that tore their biological family apart. Against this backdrop, our new family was created . . . .

"We have struggled as individuals and together—and our defeats and triumphs have been both private and collective. Perhaps our greatest accomplishment is the progress we have made in learning to communicate across deep cultural barriers, to share our fears and hopes with people whose fundamental values will remain in many ways different than our own. We have each changed in our own way, and through the process we have defined our understanding of 'family'."

To the ordinary tensions of family life, this dramatic story adds the trauma of cross-cultural adjustment—the encounter of Buddhist and Christian viewpoints—the hurt and help which lies within the structure of the traditional family.

The dramatic story of the event that brought
together an international family

SUDDEN FAMILY

Debi and Steve
Standiford
Nhi and Hy Phan

WORD BOOKS
PUBLISHER
WACO, TEXAS

A DIVISION OF
WORD, INCORPORATED

SUDDEN FAMILY

Library of Congress Cataloging-in-Publication Data

Standiford, Deborah, 1953–
  Sudden family.

  1. Stanford family. 2. Phan, Nhi, 1964– . 3. Phan, Hy, 1965– . 4. Interracial adoption—United States. 5. Inter-country adoption—United States. 6. Washington (D.C.)—Biography. 7. Handicapped children—Washington (D.C.)—Biography. 8. Vietnamese Americans—Washington (D.C.)—Biography. 9. Christian biography—Washington (D.C.) I. Standiford, Steven, 1953– . II. Phan, Nhi, 1964– . III. Phan, Hy, 1965– . IV. Title.
CT274.S76S72 1986   975.3'04'0922 [B]   86-9138
ISBN 0-8499-0567-2

Printed in the United States of America

67898FG987654321

To
Father Joseph Devlin, S.J.

the Father of the Children's Center in Songkhla Refugee
Camp, Thailand, where our family met. Father Joe lives
simply—in a single room with a bed, a desk, and a chair—
and continues to give all his time, resources, and love
to the refugees in Songkhla. The director of the Jesuit
Refugee Service told us that everywhere he travels, former refugees ask him about Father Joe and say that he
is a "true hero" to the Vietnamese people.

When we told Father Joe that we were dedicating our
book to him, he wrote that it was a "rare and precious
gift for this undeserving person, unworthy of any dedica-
tion—let alone your fine work." He explained that as he
read our book, he felt the "blood pulsing through me,
causing me to shake to my fingertips . . . Perhaps I can
explain it this way. In Thailand's tragic refugee camps
there are the stories of thousands that might be told, trage-
dies and struggles and small conquests. . . . only a few
of these stories will live. . . . But . . . at least this one
[will]."

Contents

CONTENTS

Foreword

This story is a delightful, humorous, heartwarming account of a remarkable family. Delightful—because of the intimate view of each of the four members of this unique family—two adopted Vietnamese teenage boys, Nhi and Hy Phan, and an American couple, both lawyers, in their mid-twenties with no previous experience as parents.

Humorous—as the reader is allowed a fresh view of American culture as it is experienced by a non-American for the first time. Hy describes an American staple as "a thick brown paste and a sweet red syrup between two pieces of brown bread," improved by "pouring soy sauce all over my sandwiches to make them taste better." When he observed two high schoolers kissing in the school hallway he says, "The way these lovers worked their lips reminded me so much of the fighting fish I used to own in Vietnam."

The story is heartwarming as you read of the courage and love of the boys' parents left behind in Vietnam, who refused to allow young Nhi to be an outcast from society due to his debilitating polio. They would have been delighted to see the blossoming of their two young boys into healthy, confident, unselfish personalities under the loving tutelage of Debi and Steve Standiford.

It has been my privilege to be closely involved in efforts to rescue and care for Vietnamese refugees over the last decade through my work in World Vision. So often we had heard the tragic stories of loved ones lost, maiming, sickness and suffering surrounding the entire Vietnam conflict, especially among those seeking to escape that land in search of freedom.

This story of freedom, hope and love, which Nhi and Hy Phan eventually experienced, offers needed contrast to the horrifying statistics and gruesome tales which commonly surrounded the plight of refugees. Debi and Steve allow

you to feel the intimate details of what each member of
their new family of four experienced. The reader enters
into the privacy normally shared only by close friends,
which is a particularly rare thing for a Vietnamese to do.
And this is done without losing the sense of fun, adventure
and challenge which surrounded their unusual life together.

The Vietnam people have become an important part of
the life and culture of America. Through all the agony and
trauma which we have mutually shared, it is good to be
refreshed by the vivid and moving success story of these
two young Vietnamese refugees and a courageous American
couple.

Ted W. Engstrom
President
World Vision

Introduction

Catherine Marshall tells of the ancient king who held a contest to find the perfect painting of "peace." There were many lovely entries of tranquil landscapes, but the winning picture was a scene depicting a raging storm over a mountainside. In the midst of the storm, lodged in a crevice of rock, a mother bird sat on her nest shielding her young ones. Perfect peace.

In somewhat the same way, our family has been an oasis for two boys caught in the maelstrom of war and its aftermath. Thirty years of war and a succession of totalitarian governments overcame the homeland of Nhi and Hy Phan. A way of life was destroyed. Our two sons were caught up in a chain of events that tore their biological family apart. Against this backdrop, our new family was created.

Each of us in his or her own way paid a price to be part of this family. In the process our lives have been a microcosm of what all families experience—heartbreak, laughter, misunderstanding, forgiveness. We have wrestled with inner fears and insecurities. There were normal problems between parents and teenage sons. Finally, one blow almost tore our family apart.

We have struggled as individuals and together—and our defeats and triumphs have been both private and collective. Perhaps our greatest accomplishment is the progress we have made in learning to communicate across deep cultural barriers, to share our fears and hopes with people whose fundamental values will remain in many ways different than our own. We have each changed in our own way, and through the process we have redefined our understanding of "family."

As we write these words today, around the world there are over thirty wars in progress. There are millions of children like Nhi and Hy who are watching their countries and families disintegrate in the face of overwhelming forces of hatred and destruction. We tell their story because we do not want the horror of war to be forgotten. But we tell it gently. We have no desire to glorify violence or add to the helplessness and paralyzing despair that we all feel in the face of seemingly insurmountable evils. Instead, we want to share our gratitude for our life together and the inexplicable way in which hope and love can grow out of deep wounds and suffering.

We do not know what the future holds for us. Our life together will no doubt undergo many more changes in the years ahead, particularly as Nhi's and Hy's Vietnamese family comes to America. All we know is that, by God's providence, we are a family.

Debi and Steve Standiford
Nhi and Hy Phan

SUDDEN FAMILY

1
HY

Someone Please Save My Brother!

It is like a bad dream. Nhi and I are escaping by sea from Vietnam and for the fifth time in three days our small fishing boat has been boarded by pirates. We have nothing left to give them, but they do not believe us. They treat us with great disrespect, searching everywhere for hidden gold. This time none of the women cry or faint; everyone is too tired to be afraid.

Our boat is fragile and only thirty feet long. There are more than ninety refugees on board and with pirates running around recklessly, the boat rocks from side to side. Water rushes in and it seems we will all drown. I stay down in the hold and hand up water buckets to my brother Nhi, who dumps them over the side. I see Nhi's calm, peaceful face against the sky and I think what a gentle person he is. Polio crippled him when he was a baby, and because our parents stayed behind in Vietnam, it is my duty to take care of him. We are on our way to America where doctors will fix Nhi's legs. One day soon we will play soccer together.

Suddenly a jolt from behind sends Nhi hurtling off the deck into the water. I climb up quickly, but already his shirt and pants are filled with sea water, dragging him below the surface of the Gulf of Thailand. Nhi struggles violently for air as salt water floods into his stomach. He cannot swim and death seems very near.

All around me refugees are shouting at the Thai pirate who pushed my crippled brother into the sea. Tears fill my eyes. I desperately want to dive into the ocean, but I cannot swim. I cry for help. "He is drowning! Someone please save my brother . . . !"

2
STEVE

An Adventure Begins

It was February 1980. Half a world away from Nhi's and Hy's life-and-death struggle, my wife Debi and I were practicing law in Washington, D.C. We had moved to Washington six months earlier after finishing law school at the University of Virginia, and now we were both working day and night to establish ourselves in highly competitive law firms. Debi was defending a California corporation accused of price-fixing, and she was shuttling back and forth between Washington and Los Angeles. I was litigating a federal civil rights action on behalf of an inmate who had been severely beaten in a Virginia prison.

Although our schedules left us with little time for ourselves, much less other people, Debi and I found our work exhilarating. We were also enjoying the benefits of a double income. For the first time in seven years, we were not paying tuition bills. We lived in the fashionable neighborhood of Georgetown, we bought our clothes at exclusive stores, and I sent my shirts out to be laundered. We even hired a woman to clean our apartment.

During this time, Debi and I began to attend a vibrant inner-city church. Church of the Saviour, which is pastored by the Rev. Gordon Cosby, was a congregation of 150 members who were struggling to balance their inner spiritual lives with an active outreach to others. Their ministry included a health care center, a major housing project, and job training for the poor.

One Sunday morning, Debi and I heard a moving account from Helen Cary, a woman who had just returned from the refugee camps in Thailand. She spoke of hundreds of thousands of refugees fleeing the communist regime in Vietnam. Some of the refugees left their country on foot, walking hundreds of miles through the jungles of Cambodia to Thailand. Most spent months or years saving money to buy passage on crowded, often unseaworthy vessels headed for Thailand, Malaysia, or Singapore. They became "boat people" on a one-way voyage to freedom, and the dream for which they risked their lives and possessions was a new life in America.

For many, the dream had become a nightmare. Some were captured by communist patrol boats and sent to jail. Thousands were drowned during storms, or were killed by armed pirate fishermen. Still others reached land only to have their boats towed back out to sea at gunpoint by hostile governments. Many of these boats capsized, or their passengers died of hunger and exposure.

Refugees who somehow safely reached land were crowded into makeshift refugee camps along the coast of Thailand. Most had lost all their worldly possessions. They had very little to eat and only polluted water to drink. While they waited for resettlement in the United States and other western countries, volunteers were desperately needed to teach English and help in the distribution of supplies.

A group of men and women from the Church of the Saviour would soon be leaving for the Songkhla refugee camp on the southern coast of Thailand, and as Helen finished her report, she asked each one of us to prayerfully consider joining the mission. Flight expenses would be paid by United and Tiger airlines; all we needed to provide was time and willing hands.

Debi and I were both deeply moved by the stories of the refugees' suffering. We had seen pictures of boat people on the nightly news, but it never occurred to us that there might be something more tangible that we could do besides give money. We talked together for many hours about what our response should be. Seven years earlier, while the United States was bombing Hanoi, I was a first-year cadet at West Point. At that time, I was convinced that the best course of action in Vietnam was to leave the country alone. Now, however, thousands of Vietnamese were refugees, and it was clear that they desperately needed outside help—not military aid, but food, clothes, shelter, and medicine.

In the following week, Debi and I found ourselves drawn more and more to thoughts of going to the refugee camp in Thailand. We both had vacations coming up and neither of us would lose our place on the partnership track of our law firms if we took a month's leave of absence. Besides, I was looking forward to the adventure of living in another country again. Because of my father's government service, I had already spent many years in the Far East, and going ourselves to Thailand would be much more interesting than merely sending money to refugees. We could help out in some small, on-the-spot way, and then return to our jobs, knowing we had done what we could. In short, we had nothing to lose, and an adventure to gain.

In every life, there are unexpected turning points, moments when seemingly minor choices alter our well laid plans and we find ourselves embarking on a new journey altogether. For Debi and me, the decision to go to Thailand would lead us into a far more personal involvement with Vietnamese refugees than we ever expected. And within a year, at the ripe age of twenty-six, Debi and I would be parents to two extraordinary teenage boys, Nhi and Hy Phan.

3
DEBI
On the Coast of Thailand

Steve and I were sitting in a cafe drinking a coke on our first day in Bangkok, the capital of Thailand. Steve had grown up in the Orient, but it was my first trip to a foreign country. We had two days before taking a train to the refugee camp 800 miles south of the city, but already I felt overwhelmed by the poverty around us.

Every day, hundreds of villagers from the surrounding countryside arrived in Bangkok to seek a new life in the city. They joined thousands of slum-dwellers living in tiny shacks built from scraps of cardboard, plastic, wood, or sheet metal. These fragile dwellings were crowded together on vacant lots and along "klongs"—the canals used for transportation and marketing. Public water supplies were inadequate, and people bathed, brushed their teeth, washed clothes, urinated, and swam in a mixture that looked like a dark syrup and smelled like raw, rotting sewage.

In the midst of this crush of humanity, the restaurant seemed like an oasis. I looked down at the straw in my glass and was startled to see old teethmarks and lipstick stains. "You have to clean these things before you use them," the director of our mission explained. "They've been recycled." He dipped his straw into the Coke and placed his index finger over the open end. Then he turned the straw upside down and let the Coke drain out on the cafe floor. I wondered about Coke's effectiveness as a sterilizing agent, but I was too thirsty to let my uneasiness stand in the way of a drink.

As the day wore on, I became unnerved by the crowds of people that gathered wherever we went and stared at the "furongs" (foreigners). Later, I learned that this staring was not considered rude in Thailand, but at the moment it made me feel extremely self-conscious and like the stranger that I was. All of a sudden I was attacked by a massive migraine headache. Doctors had told me that these headaches were triggered by heat, light, inadequate sleep, and a diet of low protein. I was about to embark on a month where these "triggers" would be my constant companions and I couldn't help but wonder if I had made a mistake coming to Thailand.

Despite my fears, I was genuinely excited when Steve and I finally boarded a train heading down the Malay Peninsula to the refugee camp at Songkhla. Bandits had recently attacked the train and robbed passengers, so armed guards patroled the aisles. After supper, a soldier carrying an M-16 rifle directed us to fold down our seats and go to bed. Heat, roosters, mosquitoes, and the constant tramp of soldiers made sleep difficult, and I was glad when morning finally came.

The sun rose over breath-taking countryside—thatch-roofed huts built on stilts rose out of dense, lush foliage, and tiny figures in straw hats waded through rice paddies in knee-high muddy water. Here and there were emaciated water buffaloes. Rising abruptly out of the land were the tall, stately Burmese mountains, shrouded in a mysterious fog.

In the late afternoon, we arrived at a train station near Songkhla, where we were met by a Thai college student. Chet was a friendly, hard-working young man hired by our church group. His assistance would prove invaluable to the refugee program. He directed us to a yellow Toyota pickup, and we drove toward the camp in a cloud of heat and dust. After half an hour on a road full of potholes, we rounded a bend and saw before us a beautiful ocean beach. To our left was a fertilizer factory, and the smell of its rotting fish filled the air. Straight ahead, on the beach, was a cluster of low-lying buildings surrounded by rusting barbed wire.

We stopped in front of the camp gate, and a group of thirty or more elementary-aged children came running in our direction. They pressed their noses against the fence and stuck their hands through the wire, reaching toward us. The children were deeply tanned by the equatorial sun, and they talked excitedly to one another in Vietnamese. As soon as we checked in with the guards and walked through the gate, we were surrounded by little bodies. Our arrival had been well-organized—in fifteen minutes I was scheduled to teach my first English class—so after greeting the children I hurried through the camp to find my classroom.

Six thousand people were crowded on a barren strip of beach. Most of the available space was taken up by thirty-seven open-air barracks—which I learned provided only enough space for everyone to lie down at night, sleeping elbow to elbow and sharing blankets. Here and there, people were taking afternoon naps in the barracks, and others were cooking over open fires. Children played with bits of scrap wood and metal, and everywhere there were long lines of refugees waiting for mail or immigration interviews. Other lines formed next to the handful of working latrines. The smell from the backed-up sewage was overpowering. A steady stream of garbled announcements came over a primitive public address system, and children and men were swimming in the polluted water near the shore. A few trees provided patches of shade along a sandy road running parallel to the ocean.

The children followed me into one of the barracks which functioned both as a classroom and as a refugee sleeping area and took seats on the floor near my feet. The room was crowded with dozens of squatting adults and another fifty stood outside hoping to catch some of the lesson. The barracks had a roof, but no sides. There were no desks or chairs. Some of the students had paperback books, and others had pencils or paper. A few wrote on discarded gum wrappers.

The class was "survival" English. Today, the students were learning American foods. I wrote "meat" on the board and my Vietnamese co-teacher wrote the translation "thit." I said meat loud enough for 100 people to hear me.

"Mee-eet" came the reply. I heard two syllables, the first high, the second low. "Again," I prompted. The response was drowned out by the camp PA system. "Please, again." This time there was a noticeable improvement. The class went on in this fashion for an hour, with all the students eagerly trying to repeat everything I said. They were determined to learn English and their enthusiasm was infectious. I was already feeling useful, and I was looking forward to the month we would have together.

After the class, a small group of the younger girls followed me down to the beach for an impromptu English lesson and a soda at a camp "restaurant." We sat at a table and on benches that were made from wooden planks torn off rotting refugee boats. I bought two drinks from a Vietnamese man who had purchased supplies from Thai merchants outside the camp gate, and I divided them into seven small glasses filled with crushed ice. After some coaxing, the girls shyly accepted my gift. I felt happy to be able to give them such a special treat and I was surprised how ordinary and everyday our time together seemed. My young friends, who were between the ages of six and ten, had lost everything on their boat trip, and now they were waiting in a crowded, mosquito-infested refugee camp for a chance to emigrate to a western country. Yet for a moment we laughed and sipped our sodas as if we were dining in a fancy American restaurant.

One of the children who adopted me my first day in the camp was a brown-haired nine-year-old boy who was deaf and mute. The unintelligible noises he made sounded even more foreign than the sing-song Vietnamese tones of the other children. My first thought was that I wished I knew sign language, but I soon discovered that my young friend had never been to school. So we invented our own language of gestures and facial movements. We nodded, grimaced, arched our eyebrows, pointed, and smiled. After the first day, he met me at the gate each morning and reached for my book bag with the ceremony of a hotel doorman. He would never let me carry the bag myself, and throughout the day he was seldom more than a few feet away from me wherever I went.

On my second day in camp, I visited the Children's Center, an open-air barracks for more than seventy homeless children run by Father Joseph Devlin, a Jesuit. The majority were boys sent off by their parents to start new lives in America. A few were children who had lost their mothers and fathers at sea. Two of the boys, Nhi and Hy Phan, were orphans whose parents were killed during the war.

All of the children made me feel very much at home, and the cook invited me to eat lunch with their teachers. As she filled my plate, she explained that I was lucky to eat with them that day—the menu was cooked pig's blood. I looked down at the large, dark red coagulated lumps, and I was not at all sure that I wanted such an unusual international experience. But all eyes were on me, and there was little choice but to take a bite. Since no drinks were served during the meal, there was nothing with which to wash it down, and I swallowed my portion so quickly that even to this day I cannot remember its taste. "Do you like it?" the teachers asked eagerly. I smiled bravely, and lied that it was delicious.

After lunch, we moved to the other side of the barracks for an English class taught by a twenty-one-year-old refugee, Loc Tran. On my way to the class, I noticed that the paralyzed boy, Nhi Phan, had no wheelchair, no braces, and no crutches. He was totally dependent upon his brother, Hy, for transportation, and the brother clearly took his responsibility very seriously. He bent low in front of Nhi, helped him climb on his back, and carried his brother to the class, where he gently lowered him on a wooden bench. After class, Hy repeated his labor of love, and carried Nhi to the sleeping area. The silent communication between the boys—a smile, a nod, a touch—spoke of their deep devotion to one another.

The teacher, Loc, had an astonishing grasp of English grammar and an excellent rapport with the students. His weakness was pronunciation, and after the first class, we decided to become a teaching team. I would spend my mornings at the Children's Center, helping Loc with his young students.

By our third day in camp, Steve and I had fallen into a routine. Steve bought supplies or dug wells for drinking water, and taught English classes at night. I taught English throughout the day and evening, and visited with refugees in the camp during my free time. The days sped by as I rejoiced in a strong sense of purpose and usefulness, yet struggled to adjust to the food, the equatorial heat, the extreme poverty, and the overwhelming suffering of people who were becoming my friends. Many had lost loved ones during "The Thirty Years War"—which Americans call the Vietnam War. Several men talked about their years in "re-education" (concentration) camps, where they had been imprisoned because of their prior association with the United States or the government of South Vietnam. On a meager diet of rice, they had been forced to do the work of water buffaloes—clearing fields (many of which contained concealed, unexploded mines), pulling plows, and hauling logs.

Many of the refugees in the camp had suffered unspeakably during their flight by boat across the Gulf of Thailand. A twelve-year-old girl in the Children's Center, who had been raped on her boat by armed robbers, was still unable to remember her name. A young boy in my morning class saw his father drown when their boat sank within sight of land. An elderly, educated man showed the bullet wound he received when fishermen fired into his crowded boat. And there was the beautiful eighteen-year-old girl who had been abducted by pirates and held captive in a brothel in Bangkok. After arriving in the camp she had spent her first three months sobbing in her bed. The first time she felt strong enough to talk about her experience was during a writing assignment in my advanced English class.

Every day I heard new stories. Young mothers, old men, and small children came to me and in broken English or with the help of an interpreter shared their sorrows. Never once did I find words adequate to respond to their stories. Often I wondered if my presence was useless in the face of such sadness.

An eight-year-old boy, whose name I never learned, taught me otherwise. Barefoot and dressed only in shorts, he approached me one afternoon while I was walking along the camp road. He took my hand and led me down to the beach, where he motioned for me to sit in the shade of a large tree. For about twenty minutes he spoke in animated Vietnamese, gesturing dramatically with his hands. It seemed to make little difference to him that I did not understand his language. At the end of his story, he again took my hand and led me back to where we first met. He disappeared into a crowd of refugees and I never saw him again.

I thought about this encounter for a long time afterward and I often remember this little boy when people ask me how a lawyer from America could help in a Vietnamese refugee camp. I went to Songkhla to teach English. But through this unexpected encounter, I learned that I was being called to a simpler, yet more urgent task—to listen. I never learned what this young refugee boy was trying to tell me. But I know that he found a hand to hold and a heart to listen. He did not need me to *do* anything for him; he simply needed me to *be* with him.

I was continually amazed at the resourcefulness and generosity of the refugees I met. One woman in my advanced English class was from a well-to-do, educated family. Nga had worked for U.S. AID and Shell Oil Company in Vietnam, and her English was flawless. She was presently an interpreter for a United Nations social worker and even in the middle of the squalor of the refugee camp, she was unmistakably feminine and refined.

When I asked Nga how she had supported herself in Vietnam when her husband was sent to a "reeducation camp," she replied, "I raised pigs." I could not imagine Nga as a pig farmer.

"How did you ever know what to do?" I asked in shocked admiration.

"I got a book from the library on pig farming," Nga explained matter-of-factly. My admiration deepened.

On another occasion, I received a special gift from a young girl named Trinh, who taught me that the higher qualities of kindness and mercy do not depend on life being good. Every evening, after eight hours of working in the camp, we would return to our volunteer house for dinner and a short break (Thai regulations prevented volunteers from living in the camp). When we finished eating our spicy Thai meals, we took turns washing ourselves with a hose

in the backyard. Then we raced to the truck for a return
ride to the camp. The sun was usually just going down,
but the heat lingered. In a few minutes, the effects of my
"shower" were gone. The dust from the dirt roads billowed
over the back of the truck and mixed with our perspiration
to cover us all with visible coats of grime.

One evening, in my hurry to get to the truck, I forgot
the rubber band with which I held up my long hair. There
was no time to go back, and when we reached the camp
ten minutes later, my hair was plastered to the back of
my perspiring neck.

Trinh and her friends were waiting at the gate. (More
than ever the fence seemed unnecessary; it was too hot
to move, much less escape.) Trinh wore her hair in a pony-
tail, and she was wearing a ruffled dress, the kind American
girls wear to church on Sundays. She stood out from her
friends who wore the traditional Vietnamese slacks and
loose blouses that their mothers made by altering second-
hand clothing given by our church group. Trinh had fled
with her father, but her mother was still in Vietnam.

Trinh took my hand, and we walked slowly to the classroom. She took a seat on the floor with the other children,
who stopped talking as soon as we entered the room. They
were on their best behavior because they had been shooed
away from some of my adult classes.

I stood beneath a bare hanging light bulb that attracted
tiny flying insects. They circled the air that was already
heavy with mosquitoes. Usually when I taught I held the
chalk in my right hand and swatted insects with my left,
but that night I had to hold up my hair. My right hand
did triple duty—writing, killing mosquitoes, and wiping the
sweat from my brow just before it dripped into my eyes.

I felt so miserable that it was difficult to concentrate on
my teaching. If only I had remembered my rubber band!
I knew it would be hot in Thailand, but I never imagined
it would be so hot that the absence of a rubber band would
be a major obstacle. Everyone sensed my awkwardness as
I held my hair, wrote, swatted mosquitoes, and talked.

Out of the corner of my eye, I saw Trinh pull the rubber

band out of her hair and hide it inside her closed hand. She glanced cautiously over her shoulder. A woman behind her frowned and shook her head. Trinh started to stand up, but hesitated. Then in one quick movement she handed me her rubber band and sat down again, looking at the floor.

"*Cam on* (Thank you,)" I whispered. I put the chalk on the floor. All eyes were fixed on me as I pulled my hair back and put it into the rubber band. I stood still for a moment and savored my new freedom.

There were smiles and nods of approval all around the room. No one suggested the children leave that night. My hands could return to their customary division of labor, and I squeezed Trinh's arm as I bent down to pick up the chalk. Trinh's long hair would be hot on her neck, but she had a shy smile on her face. I thought of how I had come to the refugee camp thinking I had so much to give. But in one simple gesture Trinh taught me that I was also there to receive. She gave me all she had, and it was exactly what I needed.

That night, as I returned to the volunteer house, I was aware more than ever of the division between me and the refugees. I wanted to invite Trinh to spend an evening with us, but the same regulations that prevented us from sleeping in the camp prevented her from leaving it. And no matter how much I wanted to identify with my new friends, I was an American. My citizenship shielded me from being without a country. Unlike the refugees, I could always go home. Chances were I would never have to beg another country to accept me in order to escape oppression by a cruel government. I would never be towed back out to sea in an unseaworthy boat by hostile neighbors.

Although I was torn by these thoughts, I realized that my Vietnamese friends were not. They never seemed to look down on me because I had so much more than they did. Instead, they often mentioned how much it meant to them that an American lawyer would choose to spend a vacation in the camps. They accepted me, and their acceptance seemed to be without qualification.

The truth was I had never felt so alive and so full of
energy. I regretted that our time left in the camp was so
short, and I wondered what it would be like to return home.
Could we ever go back to business as usual? Wasn't there
something more we could do? I hoped that somehow in
Washington we would find a way to continue to help our
new refugee friends.

4
NHI

A Child of War

Every day I pray to Buddha to let my younger brother Hy live one more year. I need him to take care of me. In my last life I was a bad person, and as punishment I was crippled with polio when I was one year old. Everyone who sees me knows that it is my fault that I can't walk; that is why I don't like to go places. People make fun of me, and point and laugh. But I try to be good so that in my next life I will look like everyone else.

At night I watch Hy play soccer on the beach with the other boys from the Children's Center. Hy carries me to the beach and quickly lowers me to the sand before anyone notices us. He is so small that I am heavy for him. I yell and cheer for Hy; he is one of the best players. His leg muscles are very big, and he is quick and strong. He makes the most points for his team, and the other boys like him a lot. Just like in Vietnam, where he was the leader of his "gang" in school.

My brother is smart too. He went to the best schools in Vietnam, and was always at the top of his class. I'm not smart like him. Everyone knows that polio affects the brain, and that is why I always went to a special school in Vietnam where I did not have to study very hard.

The sun has made Hy's skin dark and streaked his wavy black hair with brown. Neither Hy nor I like our dark skin because it makes us look like peasants who work in the rice fields. Hy hates his curls too because the other children call him "lai," which means a person who is not pure Vietnamese. But I like my curly hair because it is like my father's. I miss my parents a lot, and I wonder how my brother and sister are doing in Saigon.

Hy does everything for me since we escaped from Vietnam. He carries me to class and to the bathroom. He brings me buckets of water so I can bathe. And he keeps checking with the immigration people to see if we can go to America. In America, doctors will fix my legs. Then Hy and I will play soccer together. I will pass the ball to him and he will score the winning point for our team.

The problem is we are having trouble at immigration. Sometimes Hy carries me to an interview with the officials. We go behind the camp, where the sand is loose and hard to walk on, so that only a few people will see us. And every time the man says to Hy, "It is hard to find a sponsor for you, because your brother is handicapped." His words hurt me so badly. Hy slowly carries me behind the barracks and back to the Children's Center. We sit and look at each other in silence. I want to cry but the tears stay in my eyes. I know that if it were not for me, Hy would have been in America a long time ago, just like all the other children who have left the Center before us.

Sometimes when I am sad, I think of happy times in Vietnam when there was no war. When I was a small boy, I lived with my mother in a fishing village of about 500 people in Central Vietnam. My parents could not find jobs in the same town, so my mother and father lived apart for several years. During that time, Hy lived with my father. My mother was a nurse-midwife, and our one-story wooden house was divided into four small rooms where women waited to give birth or recover from delivery.

Every morning, at 4:00 A.M., the Buddhist monks who lived in a temple near our house rang a large gong to waken all the fishermen. A few minutes later, I heard the men start their small outboard engines and sail out to sea together. Sometimes I watched the lights on their boats until I fell asleep again.

When Ma woke me at 6 o'clock, she bathed me with a soft cloth and cooked a wonderful breakfast of soup and rice. We watched the sunrise as we ate. Outside our window the strong watermen pushed their bicycles. They were loaded down with buckets of fresh water from a well about half a mile outside the village. Competition was tough.

Everyone in the village wanted at least one bicycle load of clean water every morning for bathing and cooking. Business was bad for the watermen when it rained, because families collected the water that ran off their roofs.

After breakfast, Ma boiled her needles, syringes, and other instruments and put them in wet cotton in a metal box. Everyone came to see my mother, not just pregnant women, but injured fishermen and people with fevers, sores, rashes, or coughs. If they did not have money to pay their bill, they gave Ma fish or coconuts.

Sometimes pregnant women came to see my mother so they would know whether they were going to have a boy or a girl. My mother tied a piece of thread to a sewing needle, and then stuck the needle in the eraser of a short pencil. She dangled the needle and pencil above the woman's left wrist. If they moved parallel to the forearm, the baby was a boy. But if they moved perpendicular to the forearm, the baby was a girl. Everyone knew that this was a sure test, and my mother was almost always right about the sex of babies.

When lunch was over I took a nap in a hammock strung between two coconut trees and fell asleep in the shade as the breeze gently rocked me. Sometimes my grandmother visited, and sang or told me stories as I lay in the hammock. Because she was blind, she was always led by the hand by my cousin. My grandmother loved me so much, and her soft voice helped me to fall asleep.

Once when our family met together, Hy gave me my most favorite present—a red plastic toy helicopter. He had found it in a pile of junk inside a bamboo thicket, and he carefully washed it and brought it to our reunion. I took the helicopter home and replaced the missing wheels with medicine bottle caps and made propellers by whittling bamboo blades. I played with the helicopter every day for several years, and then I gave it to my younger brother.

Over these happy days, the war always cast its shadow. We never knew when our plans would suddenly change because of bombing from the sky or an invasion by the Viet Cong. We moved many times to get away from the war.

My earliest memory of the war was in 1968. Our entire family met together to celebrate the Vietnamese New Year, Tet. I always felt safer when we were all together, but this time neighbors came to say that the Viet Cong were on their way to our village. My stomach crunched inside from fear. If something happened to my family, no one would take care of me. And who knew what terrible thing might now come to be?

On the first night of Tet, we went to bed with fear. I was sound asleep when my father grabbed me and threw me on the floor. "Crawl to the basement! Quick!" I heard bullets far away, but they were quickly coming closer. I crawled dizzily to the concrete stairs. It was so dark I could not see anyone. Halfway down the stairs my father grabbed me and pulled me to the basement floor.

I could not see my mother, but I could feel her shaking. Her voice trembled as she prayed to Buddha, and in the quiet even her whispers sounded like shouting. The other women, some pregnant and some with newborn babies, joined her, and although they said different words, they all had the same meaning—Buddha, rescue us from death; save us from the fighting; protect our children and all those in our midst. If many people joined together to pray, and repeated the same prayer enough times, then Buddha would hear and rescue us from trouble.

Suddenly we heard the sound of A-K Soviet machine guns right over our heads. It was the Viet Cong. Bullets crashed into our house, and someone knocked loudly on the door with a rifle butt. Then the door was ripped open, and the machine gun fired again. Glass crashed onto the floor.

I could feel death coming. Everyone prayed silently, "Please don't walk down here." I could not hear anyone else breathing, and I knew that they too could feel death. Loud steps came closer. "Anyone here?" a voice echoed through the empty house. Feet passed by the basement opening, and then stopped. I looked up and saw that the yellow wooden cover was not over the opening. "Something, please cover us," I prayed. I lowered my eyes; I did not want to look at the man who was going to kill me. Maybe he would throw a hand grenade down or just start shooting.

But there was only a long silence, and then the steps walked toward the front door and out into the night. I leaned against the person next to me, and within a few minutes I fell asleep. When I awoke, it was still dark, and I could hear a jumble of bullets, artillery, hand grenades, and the other noises of war. Then I fell asleep again, and it was quiet.

In the morning, my father carried me upstairs. There were so many bullet holes in the front door that I could see light shining through. There was broken glass and pale pink china on the floor, and bullet holes all over the walls and cabinet. Our Vespa motorscooter had been shot through many times, and even my bed had holes in it.

Ma said it was a good thing we forgot to cover the opening to the basement. In the dark, the yellow cover would have attracted the soldier's attention, but as it was he didn't notice the black hole right at his feet. Something must have covered his eyes. And Buddha or an angel kept the babies from crying. It was the only night when none of them cried.

The war came many times again. American soldiers rode by our house in jeeps or trucks, and I could see hair on their chests when they took off their shirts. The soldiers ate food from metal cans, and they were very friendly to me, even though they knew I couldn't walk. They gave me boxes of small, round colored chocolates called "W-W's" * and pieces of peppermint-tasting rubber called "sum-gum."

Almost every day jeeps came by carrying wounded soldiers. They had no one to comfort them and nothing covered their bodies. They were in so much pain, and sometimes their blood dripped on the street in front of our house. Most of them were too badly hurt to tell from their faces whether they were Vietnamese or American. But I knew the big bodies were Americans and the smaller ones Vietnamese.

One evening a jeep rushed by even more quickly than usual. A man with no legs lay on the jeep floor. He was covered with blood. No cover gave him any privacy. I turned away so that my stare would not embarrass him.

---

* "M & M's."

The Vietnamese soldiers were not friendly like the Americans. All the women hid when they came because they were afraid. One day I heard a young student begging an officer not to hit him. "Why haven't you registered to be in the Army?" the officer demanded. He threw the student to the ground and kicked him. Then he slapped him across the face many times. The student did not dare to run because two soldiers were pointing their M-16's at him.

People on the street stood some distance away and watched the beating. They looked sad, but they knew there was nothing they could do. When the lieutenant finished hitting the boy, he lay in the dirt without moving. Then two soldiers grabbed him and dragged him away to the army base.

One time, when the fighting was very bad and we had been hiding in our tunnel for more than two weeks, we heard that B-52's were going to bomb our town. We had to leave our house very quickly. My mother packed up a few clothes and some food in baskets and tied them to the ends of a bamboo pole. She carried the pole while my father carried me.

We ran past the school where Hy was a student. Suddenly I heard an A-K Soviet gun. I looked back and saw many people running in the same direction we were. The women wore black pants and white shirts, and the men had on pants or shorts. Everyone was wearing cone-shaped straw hats to protect them from the sun, and many people were barefoot. I wondered if they left home so quickly that they didn't have time to put on their sandals.

Grenades exploded around us, and we heard the firing of tanks. Everyone ran off the dirt road and fell down in the tall, thick grass. No one moved. Mosquitoes were biting my legs, and sweat tickled my nose, but there was nothing I could do. A helicopter flew overhead, and many people jumped up and started running. But my family stayed still in the grass until all the noises stopped.

When we got back on the road, we went even faster. My mother kept saying *"Gap, gap"* (Hurry, hurry), and Hy's legs were so short he had to run to keep up with us. There was smoke all around, and noise from guns and bombs.

"Are you tired?" my father asked.

"Yes," I said.

My father laughed. "But I'm doing all the walking for both of us!"

"Yes, but you go so fast that I have to use all my muscles to hold onto you!" We laughed together. My father could always find a reason to make a joke.

In the next few years, I moved back and forth between the house of my mother and the house of my father. I began to understand how difficult it was to be a handicapped person in Vietnam. Families are embarrassed to have a crippled person in the house, and many times they kick their handicapped child out on the streets. If the child is old enough, he might be forced to become a beggar. If he is young, sometimes he goes to an orphanage. My own family was different; they paid me special attention and did everything for me so that I would feel loved.

I will never forget the first time I saw a handicapped beggar. Our family was eating at a Pho restaurant—Pho is my favorite soup, a spicy broth thick with pork and noodles—and a man with no legs scooted into the restaurant. He pulled himself along on a board tied beneath his thighs, and his hands were wrapped in cloth. His clothes were greasy and he wore a long beard.

"Why does he walk like that? Why is he so dirty?" I asked in a shocked voice. My mother told me not to worry, the man was fine. She changed the subject and told me a funny story, while my father jumped up and ran over to the beggar. He gave him some money, and then walked him out of the restaurant. But I worried about that man for a long time. I was afraid I might become like him if my family died.

When I was five years old, a Buddhist nun came to our house. She was mute, but she wrote out a message for my mother explaining that she came from an orphanage that cared for handicapped children. If I went with her, they would give me medicine for my legs, and I could learn to read and write. I did not want to go away, and I was glad that my mother told the nun I was staying home.

After that, I began to ask my mother many times if she was going to send me away. One time, she cried and took me on her lap. She hugged me tightly and said that she would always take care of me. She did not want me to live in a lonely orphanage. My father said the same thing. One day he wrote me a letter, and it read like a poem. "Son, I love you, but since you are young it is hard to express. Your mother and I will work hard to save money for you. We will not drink coffee or eat fancy dinners. Then if we die, you will have money to survive." Although my father wrote this to console me, when I understood that my parents might leave me some day, I was very afraid. It had been a secret fear for a long time, but I did not know that they too were afraid and preparing for the future.

One day, my father told me we were going on a trip. I seldom went anywhere, and I was full of excitement. We traveled many miles south on a small bus, and I felt so special because I was the only son who had the privilege of traveling with my father. Soon we came to a long, one-story building with a covered walkway. There was a beautiful yard with many flowers, and I saw children playing games. Some of the children had no legs. My father talked to a man who looked like a doctor, but I did not understand what they were saying.

My father and I spent the night in a big room with many children. Our beds were straw mats on the floor. In the morning, we folded them up, and my father said, "Nhi, I am going for breakfast. Wait here; I will be back soon."

The whole day passed, and my father did not return. At night a Catholic sister put me into a bed with wooden bars on the sides. In the middle of the night, I needed to go to the bathroom, but I could not get over the bars. I went in the bed and felt so embarrassed. This would never happen at home, because we kept a bowl by the bed.

My father did not come back the next day either. I felt nervous being around so many strangers, and I wondered why my father had left me in such a place. It looked like the orphanages I had heard about, but orphanages were for children whose parents were dead or did not want them. My parents were alive and loved me very much. My mother had promised she would never send me away.

Many days passed, and my father did not return. I learned

that my new home was called the Orphan's Hospital. The sisters were kind, and for several weeks they exercised my legs every day. But then they stopped. I think they gave up, because no matter how hard they worked, I still could not move my legs.

Every night I sat on the smooth concrete of the covered walkway and watched the road where my father walked away. I often planned ways to escape and crawl home. But how could I crawl all the way to our village? So many days passed, I thought I would never see my father and mother again.

One day Americans came to the orphanage and at dinner time a sister announced that there would be a special treat in our rice bowls. When I looked down at my steaming portion I was expecting candy or chocolate, but instead I saw a brown oily paste.* I did not know what it was, but the taste was wonderful. Usually I was too sad to eat, but this time I had a second portion and then asked for more. The nun said I was too small to eat so much, and gave me only half a bowl. I ate slowly, so that it would last a long time.

Six months after my father went away, my mother came to visit me. When she called my name, I crawled to her, and she ran to me and held me tightly in her arms. She cried and cried. She stayed at the orphanage all day and all night, and I was so happy. All my friends who really were orphans were happy too. But the next day, my mother told me she had to leave. She promised to return. I thought I would never stop crying after she left. I sat and looked down the same road where my father, too, had walked away.

A few days later, I heard my father's voice. He came into my room, and with his strong arms, he picked me up and threw me into the air. He was so happy, he was laughing. We packed up a few things in a paper bag, and my father carried me out the door. I think my mother told him that it made her too sad to see me at the orphanage.

When we arrived home, Hy and my older brother Tri asked me, "Where have you been?" I did not tell them

---

* peanut butter

about the orphanage, because I thought that would make them sad. But I told them about a room where we bathed that had pipes with water coming out. They did not believe me. I also told them about the brown American food. We laughed and tried to guess what it was.

When I was nine years old, our family moved together to Saigon, and I went to school. Classes started at 6:30 in the morning and lasted until noon. At 9:30 there was a half-hour break for recess, and all the children, except me, went outside to play. I felt lonely. The children never invited me to play with them, but that was okay, because I watched them play. I had to pull myself up to the window and hold onto the shutter the entire recess. But I loved seeing the boys play hide and seek and the girls play "chopsticks," a game like jacks except you bounce a ball and try to pick up chopsticks.

The worst part of school was the bathroom. The students were too small to carry me there, and the area around the toilet was always wet. To avoid embarrassment, no matter how hot it was or how thirsty I became, I never drank any water before or during school.

One day I had to go to the bathroom very badly. The pain grew worse and worse, and I kept twisting in my seat. Everyone could see that I was in big trouble, but the teacher ignored me and continued to teach her lesson.

When I could wait no longer, I slid out of my seat and crawled to the toilet. In the bathroom, my pants were soaked by all the water and urine on the floor. I relieved myself and crawled back to my seat, dragging my legs and wet pants behind me. I could hear the boys in the class laughing at me, and my face was hot and sweating all over. I looked down at the floor to hide my shame. The teacher did not say anything but continued to teach her lesson.

During these years, there were many times that our family went hungry. We had our small store, my mother continued to nurse patients, and my father drove a pedicab—a taxi propelled by foot pedals—but still money was scarce. Somehow, even when there was very little food, Ma and Ba spent money trying to find doctors or witches who could heal my legs. One time a woman put burning incense inside ginger root and placed it on my joints. The incense burned through the ginger and then scorched my skin. My father held me down, and I cried and yelled, but the pain did not stop.

Another time, my mother sold her favorite necklace to hire a Kung Fu expert who was skilled in healing polio victims. For several months, he came to our house one night each week. He pushed on my back with great strength, and built parallel bars for me to hold onto while I wore heavy weights on my shoes. Once he made me eat food for pigs, and another time he covered my back with sticky leaves for forty-eight hours. When the leaves came off, there were red welts all over my crooked back.

It made me feel sad that so much money was wasted on cures that never worked, and sometimes I thought about killing myself so I would not be such a burden to my family. I knew that if I died I would be reincarnated with strong legs, and my family would have more to eat. One time I took the iodine from Ma's medicine box, and crawled away to drink it. But at the last minute I changed my mind. I was not brave enough to do it.

5
HY

When Death Was Near

Buddha has been good to us. Almost every day I pray to Buddha to let me live one more year, and now I am fourteen years old. It is a miracle that Nhi and I have lived so long, and that we are safe in this refugee camp.

Our first month here we slept on the beach, but now we are living in a wonderful center for children. We have a straw mat to sleep on, and the roof shelters us from the hot sun during the day, although there are too many holes to stay dry when it rains. Nhi and I are learning English so that we can go to America. It is good to be safe and have hope, but sometimes I almost give up because the immigration officials have turned us down so many times.

I promised my parents I would take care of Nhi, and if anything happens to him, it will be my fault. The immigration people say Nhi cannot go to America because he cannot walk, but somehow I must get us there. My father said Americans are very good people who have excellent technology for operations. I know they can fix Nhi's legs in America, if we can only find a sponsor.

Nhi and I have survived too much danger together to lose out now. We made it through the Tet offensive and then spent two weeks in 1972 hiding in a tunnel during Mua He Do Lua—The Summer Red with Fire. We were in a small town near My Lai when the fighting started. Bullets awakened us in the middle of the night, and everyone in the house crawled down a ladder into a narrow, three-foot high tunnel dug out of the earth. The red ants were biting, but my older brother Tri said it was better to be bitten than to be killed. I was very afraid and prayed to Buddha, "Please let me live for two or three more years. Let me be ten years old before I leave the earth." In the dark, I tried to find Tri. My hand touched his feet, and I locked my fingers in his toes to make sure he would always be there. Then I closed my eyes and fell asleep.

All the next day, we heard bombs exploding. The tunnel shook and dirt dropped on our heads. Several neighbors joined us in the tunnel, and I felt less lonely and afraid. But my mother had been working as a midwife in another village, and she was not with us. Nhi kept asking Tri and me if our mother was coming back. We quickly answered, "Yes." But then we pondered deeply his questions. I wondered if we would ever see our mother again.

Later in the same week, when my father went upstairs to get a blanket, he saw Viet Cong marching past our house. That night I first tasted liquid fear. It was so quiet in the tunnel, we could have heard a mosquito fly by. Suddenly, there were steps directly overhead, and no one was breathing. I knew we would be killed as soon as they found us. But just like the night in the Tet offensive, the footsteps went away and did not come back. Buddha had saved us again.

In the second week there was a lull in the fighting, but my father made us stay in the tunnel. During this time, two neighboring men went upstairs to cook some rice for their families. A short while later, one of their young sons came running back, "Dr., Dr., come save my father!" My father was not a real doctor, but he had received some medical training. He ran to our neighbor's house; it had just been hit by a "canh nong"—heavy ground artillery. My father found that one of the men was already dead, but even though he knew there was no life, he gave him a shot to comfort his family. The other man had lost part of his brain and was bleeding badly. My father gave him a pain killer shot, but he could not keep him from dying.

During this time, most of our neighbors decided to leave the village. My father had heard rumors of a flood, and he thought our family would be scattered in an evacuation, so we stayed behind in the tunnel. Later we heard that some of our neighbors drowned while trying to cut across a flooded rice field, and others were shot down by helicopters.

After two weeks, the Viet Cong were beaten back, and my mother, who had stayed on the border of the fighting zone, followed the South Vietnamese army back to our town. Soon we were all together again, and we celebrated our reunion with a big party. While we were eating, an old woman with dirty white hair and a curved back came to the door asking for money. She looked like the pictures of angels in Buddhist books; sometimes Buddha sends angels disguised as poor people to test whether people will share their food or money. My mother gave the woman some rice and a large piece of pig. We thought the woman would return in a few days, because we had been able to give her so much, but we never saw her again. My parents decided that she was an angel.

Because there was so much fighting, my family moved to Saigon the next year to look for a safer life. In the spring the South Vietnamese government announced that it had received a huge load of supplies from America. "Now that our allies have given us many more guns and jeeps, we will kick out the communists just like that!" The news was so hopeful.

But then in April, 1975, the communists won the war. They set up a government to help change the "savage conditions" which they said the southern government had created. Soldiers and officers of the south were told they had to spend "only ten days" in special camps to learn the new system. But instead, they were kept in concentration camps for indefinite periods. Laws were passed allowing the government to seize private property, and "rich" people were resettled in barren provinces, where they were expected to survive on the land. Only a small percentage made it; the rest crept back to Saigon, where they had lost everything.

Most people in Saigon saw only a bleak future for their children. Many could not help but accept this fate, but those who had enough money or gold sent their children to foreign countries by any means they could find. My own parents were hoping our whole family could escape to America, but it cost several bullions of gold to buy passage on one of the small fishing boats illegally leaving Vietnam. Just before the fall of Saigon, my mother considered putting Nhi on a plane flying handicapped orphans to America, but Nhi, who was now eleven years old, did not want to go alone. Buddha was watching out for him, because that plane crashed before it even left Vietnam.*

Life in South Vietnam was not easy, and by 1979, my mother and father had saved enough money to send our oldest brother Tri to America. He left by boat, and although my mother told him to send a telegram as soon as he reached land we did not hear from him. Weeks went by, and everyone worried, especially my mother. She was absent-minded and spoke about things that made no sense. When she realized this, she would beg our pardon, and then go on to another subject. After a while, she always ended with the same sentence, "I wonder where Tri is now!"

We imagined how Tri might have survived and gotten to shore, but could not find a way to let us know. We talked to our relative who helped arrange his escape to get some soothing. My mother even went to card readers and fortune tellers, and paid a great deal of money to hear some "good news." It relieved her for a few hours at most. She repeated the news to us, but then felt worried and tired again.

Although at the end of the day my mother was exhausted, she never stopped praying to Buddha, not even one single night. She spent at least a half hour asking for Tri's salvation and a letter with good news. It seemed as if this would continue as long as we lived.

During the eight years we had lived in Saigon, the mailman had never stopped at our house, not one single time. For days we had been hopeful and tense when he passed our house. But still he never stopped.

None of us suggested that Tri was dead, but it seemed to me that the idea grew one day after another. Our family members started to move to different corners of the house during dinner to escape conversation. We ate in frozen silence.

Customers started to buy less food at our store, and the

---

* In April, 1975, a plane carrying Vietnamese children to the United States crashed soon after take-off. More than 100 children died.

income decreased every day. Nhi, the family cashier, did not have much work to do. He borrowed books to keep him company. One day he was so absorbed in a novel that he did not even notice a special person standing in front of him. The mailman had stopped! Our mother opened the letter with shaking hands. "A long letter . . . Tri's handwriting!" She cried with joy, and with the whole family circled around her, she read the good news that Tri had arrived safely in a refugee camp in Indonesia. It was one of the happiest moments our family ever knew.

A year later, while Tri was still in the same refugee camp, my mother took me aside and said it was now time for Nhi and me to go to America. I was fourteen and Nhi was sixteen; we could join our brother Tri and some day the three of us would bring the rest of our family to America.

I was anxious to leave. I was in a good school, but only 50 percent of the students would be allowed to continue their education after the ninth grade. Children of communists were given priority, and my parents were not communists. I knew I would get a good education in the west, and I would not have to worry about being drafted into the army. Although I wanted to become a soldier, a heroic and famous one, I did not want to fight for the communists. And most boys from South Vietnam were sent to fight the Khmer Rouge in Cambodia. Many youths had already been killed there. Some had escaped from the army en route to battle, but they were forced to hide inside their houses all the time so they would not be detected.

It was also good for Nhi to leave. The Buddhist spirit that made my neighbor's arm write special messages had predicted that a doctor in the west would help him walk. I tried to picture what it would be like when Nhi stood up straight and took his first steps on his new legs. It would be the greatest moment of our lives.

My one fear was that the communists might plant a bomb on our ship. A classmate of mine and his family had died in an explosion on their boat, and survivors thought the bomb had been planted by communists trying to discourage people from leaving Vietnam. What if something happened and I died, but Nhi lived? Who would carry him? Who would take him to the hospital? I could not stand to think of Nhi crawling in America. Americans would laugh at him and curse his family for not taking care of him. Nhi could not survive without me.

My mother told us we were leaving Vietnam only two weeks before it was time to go, and she gave me a picture of an American advisor, Mr. Joe, who had worked in our village. She told me to look for Mr. Joe when I got to America, and ask him to sponsor the rest of our family. Nhi recounted how Mr. Joe used to give him candy and throw him high in the air. I looked closely at the photograph and tried to memorize the man's face. He was bald, big, and smiling. He was dressed in an army uniform, and he was sitting with Vietnamese men at a party table full of soft drinks, beer, and food. I hoped I would run into him in America soon.

But two days later, my mother came back from a visit with a relative with different advice. The relative, who helped arrange our escape, had said there were too many refugees in the camp, and it was getting more difficult to get to America. "You must try to be adopted by Americans," my mother said. "Tell them your own parents are dead. Say that we died in the Summer Red with Fire. Don't tell them about Tri or anyone else. And give me back the picture of Mr. Joe."

I handed my mother the picture; now, I hoped I would never see Mr. Joe in America. He would ask me about my family and our secrets would be disclosed. The CIA agents, who were excellent investigators (I had seen them on TV), would certainly arrest us and send us home to jail. Our lives would be miserable; by any means, I must avoid that man.

On my last day of school, I regretted that I could not come right out and say good-bye to my friends. I tried a subtle farewell with my friend Hoa, who was loved by everyone. She was always class monitor or president, and the teachers liked her so much that they always let her write the lessons on the blackboard. Her handwriting was beautiful.

I respected Hoa a lot. She was mature and beautiful, and

her eyes were large and bright. She was smart too. I wanted to tell her I was going away, but it was not allowed. So I sat down next to her and said, "Chi (older sister) Hoa, you are so beautiful!"

"Don't tease me," she said, while smiling.

I took a breath. "Will you give me a lock of your hair?"

"That's silly," she remarked and then turned to a new subject. I never got a lock of her hair.

The night we left home, our family sat down at the table to eat our last meal together. Now there were six of us; in the morning there would only be four. My sister would eat breakfast and go to school. My father would drive the pedicab, and my brother, who was only seven years old, would stay home with Ma. My cap would still be hanging on the wall, but at noon time Nhi and I would not return.

"Eat up so you won't be hungry tonight," Ma said. My mother was never too busy to cook for us and we were never too full to eat what she prepared. Whenever there was not enough food, Ma gave up her share and said she had eaten enough. Often she ate the leftover or the almost-spoiled food and served us the rest of the newly cooked dishes. She never wanted her children to be hungry or poorly fed.

After dinner, we lit sticks of incense and kneeled to pray before the altar. "Buddha, protect my sons from harm and bring them safely to land," my mother prayed. "Oh highest of souls, give them success in education and help heal Nhi's legs." We all bowed and touched our foreheads on our opened hands that rested on the floor. Then Ma gave Nhi and me a sacred yellow cloth to protect our lives. It had long winding black lines, and holes had been drilled in it by incense. The cloth had been blessed by a woman who belonged to an especially sacred faith. In the past I resented the large sums of money which Ma lavished on the supernatural when there was not enough food to eat, and I begged her not to spend her money on special prayers. But tonight, knowing the religious woman had blessed my trip and my life, I approved Ma's offering.

I could not say good-bye to my younger brother; we were afraid he might slip and tell the neighbors. Nhi gave him a last "horsey ride," and I picked him up to smell his cheeks. This is the Vietnamese custom of kissing; it shows the acceptance of the other person's skin odor. Tomorrow when my brother wanted to ride my bike or take a nap in my bed, I would not be there. I wondered if I would ever see him again.

With Nhi on my handlebars, Ma and I rode our bicycles to the house of our relative where we would spend the night. Ma had packed two small grocery bags, and Nhi and I each had two shirts, a sweater, and two pairs of pants and shorts, as well as a toothbrush, some toothpaste, and my English textbook. Ma also packed some dried food for us to eat on our trip to America. The trip might take three days or a week, and we did not know if there would be food on the boat.

Our relative was very rich and very big. He was in his fifties, with gray hair and wrinkles, and everything about him commanded respect and obedience. When he invited us into his house, he immediately asked us if we were ready to escape. "You must be patient and strong when you are on the boat," he warned. "You must be confident." Then he showed me the perfectly straight line on his left palm. "It shows single-mindedness and unyieldingness," he declared, his voice sounding with pride.

What a man! I thought. I wondered if these two characteristics helped him earn his great wealth.

We said good-bye to Ma, and I studied her face so that I would never forget it. She looked older, with more wrinkles than a few years before. Her lips shook and tears filled her eyes. "Good-bye, my sons. Have a safe and peaceful trip, and telegraph home immediately. Be good boys on foreign lands; no one will help you if you are bad."

"Sleep well, Ma," I said.

"I wish you peace, Ma," said Nhi.

Ma rode slowly away on her bicycle. She was wearing a faded green blouse that made her look very poor, and she seemed short and humped over. Many years of hard labor had gradually tired her backbone, so it rested by bending forward slightly. As I watched her pedal away, I thought of all the many things I would buy for her after I got to

America. I would send home soap, radios, fans, and toys. I'd buy a TV and a car, and a house for Ma. Houses were plentiful in America. I had seen postcards of huge mansions, and Ma had always wanted to live in a house with several floors. A fortune teller once predicted that Ma would live in a big house in 1982; I was certain that by then I would have enough money to buy whatever kind of house Ma wanted.

6

HY

Escape Across the Water

Early the next morning, while the stars and the moon were still shining, we said good-bye to our relative. He reminded us to say we were orphans, and he gave us new names. Changing our names would protect our parents and our own lives, and then the Americans would not know that our mother and father were alive. "Americans only adopt younger children," our relative added. "So you must also say you are only nine and thirteen years old. These Americans are the most naive of people, and they will believe everything you say." I admired our relative's thinking. How lucky we were that he helped us!

We boarded the bus and a policeman checked our tickets. He saw that they had been purchased on the black market, and forced us to get off the bus and follow him to the station. I was afraid we were going to be thrown in jail, but he only made us buy a new ticket. Then we had to wait for a new bus.

It was just the first of many setbacks. When we finally arrived in a small coastal town eight hours later, we learned that our trip had been canceled. It was thought that the communists had discovered our group's escape plan. Several days later we returned to the coast, only to be turned back again, this time for unknown reasons.

Finally, on our third try, we boarded a small fishing boat, which had been disguised as a merchant boat. There were vegetables on the roof and sides, fresh fish exposed at the front, and tangled nets left hanging like bushes in the back. There were seven passengers, the pilot and his son, and a small, weak engine. Before the sun rose, we headed out to sea.

47

Our plan was to meet a larger escape boat, but one mile out into the ocean, the outboard motor suddenly stopped. The fisherman began to row with his oars, and the rest of us came out of hiding to row with our hands. There was joy in each one of us as we sensed that freedom was not far away, and for a long time we rowed without even feeling tired.

But by noon we still had not found the bigger boat. We drank the last bit of water, and then I tried to resist the killing thirst by sucking my tongue. It was not long before it gave me no more water. As the sun beat down on our heads, I began to feel faint.

Finally we spotted the other boat. It took us some time to catch it, and while we were in close pursuit, a woman on the boat strangled a chicken and hung it over the side as an offering to Buddha. We all bowed our heads as she said a short prayer. Then she threw the dead chicken aside and we all continued rowing with our hands.

When we came to the side of the boat, I was surprised to see it was only thirty feet by ten feet. I thought it must be taking us to a third boat which could carry many passengers. But there was no other vessel. Nhi and I said good-bye to our first "pilot" and his son and then boarded the boat. I had the mixed feelings of a boy who was leaving the place where he was born and raised to go to a faraway land.

Nhi and I joined 89 other refugees, and we were assigned to a space in a cabin that was so low we could not even stand up. The mechanic started the engine, and the boat moved ahead in the water. Several seagulls attempted to fly toward the southwest sky, but the mighty wind was against them. They struggled, made loud cries, and then changed their course to the right. We were surrounded by water, deep blue water, and our fates were turned over to Buddha. I crouched down with Nhi and thanked Buddha that we had made a safe trip. If only my parents could know that we were already on the escape boat! I felt homesick as I imagined the celebration that would take place; a pig would be killed, and everyone would eat until they felt full.

As we passed Phu Quoc Island, the last piece of Vietnamese land, eight Russian fishing trawlers suddenly began to give chase. Fortunately, they were pulling so many fish that we outdistanced them after awhile. The victory was so glorious nothing could compare with it. Everyone rejoiced, and Nhi and I prepared for a peaceful sleep through the night. But all of a sudden a woman's voice cried out in merriment, "American ship!" Nhi crawled outside of the cabin, and I stood beside him, holding our two bags in readiness to board the approaching boat.

As the ship came closer, everyone became suddenly quiet. The sailors on the deck certainly did not look like Americans. Their hair had grown past their shoulders and they wore headbands on their foreheads. Their clothes were torn, and their beards were long and tangled with pieces of food. Each of them was armed with a pistol and a sharp knife.

"Pirates!" The man next to me cried.

While one pirate remained on his boat with a gun pointed toward us, five others jumped into the water and swam toward us. They boarded our boat and ordered us to raise our arms above our heads. They pushed their guns into the refugees' stomachs, and took watches, rings, necklaces, and earrings. As darkness came, they worked faster. Finally, they returned to their boat with a large bag of other people's possessions. Nhi and I sat still, looking at one another, and trying to share our miserable feelings.

As the sun went down, the wind reached its full power. It seemed to warn us not to go any further. It struck the cabin and the sides, and sent water to slap the weak planks, almost breaking them. The waves were bigger than ever, and our little boat rocked violently and several times almost tipped over. The front rose high above the oncoming waves, and then dipped very low as the waves passed. Nhi and I crouched in the cabin and shivered in the cold. We could not get our extra shirts from our bags because there was no space to move.

"Help, a leak!" shouted a voice in the dark. The mechanic ordered everyone out on the deck, and the sea spray made us colder than ever. I could hear Nhi's teeth banging against

one another. Several strong men threw three bags of rice
overboard to make their way to the leak. I had never seen
anyone throw food away before, and I was stunned. By
the time they reached the leak, there was only one bag
of rice left. The leak was sealed with a special rubber, and
we returned to the cabin for a few hours sleep.

In the morning we were awakened by Thai pirates. They
boarded the boat and searched every person, tearing our
shirts, and inspecting our whole bodies. By the time they
left, we were devastated. We had lost almost everything,
and we still had a long way to go.

We were attacked by pirates three more times. Once
the pirates took several women onto their boat and kept
them in their cabin for a long time. They ordered us all
on their boat for inspection, but Nhi was left behind. The
two boats were tied together, but our boat began to drift
away. I worried that the pirates' rope would break and I
would never see Nhi again. But finally the current brought
the vessels together, and we were returned to our own
boat.

During the last attack, when we were only a half mile
from the coast of Thailand, thirty men boarded the boat
and began searching wildly for hidden treasures. We tried
to tell them we had nothing left, but they did not believe
us. The boat began to rock back and forth, and ocean water
rushed in. I grabbed a bucket and scooped it full of water.
Nhi poured it back into the sea, and as we scooped and
poured, I prayed that the boat would not sink.

Suddenly I felt a sharp swaying of the boat and heard a
big splash. Nhi was gone. I shouted with all my strength
"Help! Help!" I wanted to jump into the water, but I could
not swim. A young pirate climbed onto the boat; he had
grabbed hold of Nhi as the boat swayed and they both had
fallen over together. But only the pirate came back.

Nhi floated to the surface, and a woman on the edge of
the boat grabbed his foot. At the same time, a pirate dove
into the water and helped Nhi out. Nhi was pale and choking, and I rushed to give him a big hug. I made sure that
we both sat securely in the boat. Nhi was angry to be locked
inside my arms, and yelled, "Let me loose." But I did not
let him go.

When the last pirates left, we turned the boat back around and headed for the Thai coast. We had been traveling for three days under the hot sun; now the ocean breeze seemed to cool my whole body and my soul. We reached land in less than half an hour, and as soon as the boat ran aground, I jumped in the water. Everything seemed to turn in a circle. I wobbled like a drunken man, and staggered to a shady area on the beach before I fell down. *This is a miracle,* I thought, and I whispered a prayer to Buddha.

We were soon surrounded by a group of curious Thai villagers. I felt proud and happy that so many people we didn't even know came to welcome us. The men tore our boat apart, looking for hidden treasure, but a kind woman gave Nhi a cooked ear of corn. The steam rising into the air and the large, yellow kernels made me so hungry. Nhi took a bite and passed the corn around. It was the best food I ever ate.

Trucks came and took us to a nearby police station. We took a bath in a stream close to the station, and as Nhi and I sat on the bank waiting for our shorts to dry, a Thai man came to us and gave Nhi a giant piece of cloth. He showed Nhi how to wrap it around him Thai-style, and then went away. We were so grateful for this kind act.

In the evening, Thai policemen brought us forms to fill out. They asked for simple information—name, age, family members—and I shuddered at the inevitable discovery of our false identity. We were safe for a moment, but the CIA had lie-detectors and other modern equipment. Perhaps it would be only a matter of time before we were sent to jail or tortured.

We were at the police station for two weeks. One day a man hired me to wash his motorcycle, and then a baker paid me ten *baht* (50¢) to work for ten hours in his store. Nhi and I were unanimous in how to spend this first money; we bought a Coke. We drank it so fast, our stomachs were full of gas, but it had the real taste. It was as wonderful as we remembered. On another day, I went fishing with a friend I had met on the boat. We made our own poles, and caught over fifty small white fish from the stream where we bathed. My friend's mother fried the fish and made a delicious sauce.

After many days, trucks came and drove us all to a refugee camp called Songkhla. The camp was so crowded that for the first month we had to sleep on the beach. At night it was very cold, and we had no blankets or warm clothing. When it rained we tried to find a dry spot in the camp's Buddhist temple. But sometimes we got there too late, and the temple was already full.

Every day the United Nations gave us some rice and small canned sardines in red sauce. Then a family in one of the barracks allowed us to move in with them. Finally we were dry and warm. But then a fat man in the family started to make fun of Nhi's legs. After a few days, he ordered us to go away. I hated that man, but there was nothing I could do.

Fortunately, the Children's Center opened up the next day. The man in charge was an American priest named Father Joe. I carried Nhi on my back, and we stood in a long line of children waiting to see Father Joe. I wondered if a Catholic priest would want to help two Buddhist boys. Finally, it was our turn. Father Joe was very tall and strong. He had lots of gray hair, and his face was red from the sun. He wore black pants and a black shirt, and when he talked with us he smiled. He gave us a bag of white bread, the kind that Vietnamese love, and then he gave us some Thai money. He said we could stay at the Center with the other children.

Nhi and I were happy to sleep indoors. Sometimes I lay awake at night when the mosquitoes were biting, or when it was hot, and I thought about what would happen to us. No Vietnamese in America would adopt us because Nhi was handicapped. But American parents would not speak Vietnamese so how would they understand us? Maybe we would live in the refugee camp for the rest of our lives.

This month there is a new teacher in the Children's Center. Her name is Mrs. Debi from America, and she follows the Vietnamese custom of taking off her shoes before she enters the Center. Once her husband, Mr. Steve, came to our class. He gave Mrs. Debi a kiss; I was very surprised. All the girls were embarrassed and turned their heads away. In Vietnam it is a sign of disrespect to kiss a woman in public. I do not know why, but it gave me a good feeling.

This morning, Father Joe told me that Mr. Steve and Mrs. Debi want to talk to me. I am very worried. Maybe I am in trouble. My English is not very good, and I will not know what to say. Sometimes I wish we had never left Vietnam.

7
STEVE
A Family Is Born

Even before I fell in love with Debi, one of the qualities that I deeply admired was her almost childlike idealism. Among her most basic beliefs seemed to be the conviction that, with enough love, all human wounds could be healed. It was a view of the world which I found at once endearing and exasperating.

In college, Debi dreamed of having enough money to buy houses for the ghetto children at the day care center where she was a volunteer. When we were dating, she confided to me that her favorite childhood story was *Jo's Boys* (a sequel to *Little Women*), in which a young woman raises a houseful of orphaned and needy children. That seemed to me a noble but highly impractical way of life.

Now, three days before we were scheduled to leave the refugee camp in Songkhla, the specter of *Jo's Boys* returned. Just as I was falling asleep, Debi turned to me and with an enigmatic smile on her face said that she wanted to adopt two boys living in the Children's Center. *Oh, no,* I thought, *here we go again.* Outwardly I laughed. "Okay, let's adopt all the children at the Center. There are only 75 of them."

Debi insisted that she was serious. There were two boys at the center, Nhi and Hy, to whom she felt especially drawn. Nhi was handicapped and had to be carried to class by his brother. Their parents were killed during the war, and Debi had a strong feeling that God was calling us to be their new mother and father. She had been talking to Father Joe and to Terry Flood, a volunteer from our church, who had several adopted children. Everyone was enthusiastic.

The whole idea seemed crazy to me. Debi and I were both only twenty-six, and adoption would be an enormous responsibility. We had already agreed to sponsor Debi's co-teacher, Loc, and help him in his adjustment to life in the United States. He would be sleeping in our living room (we had only one bedroom) for a few months while he looked for a job and went to school, but our responsibility would be limited. Adopting children, on the other hand, would mean becoming financially, legally, and emotionally responsible for two other human beings. The sacrifice of time and energy would last at least for several years, and perhaps even for the rest of our lives.

And these weren't just *any* kids. We didn't speak the same language or share the same culture. They were half grown, and I wasn't even old enough to be their father. We might never feel like a family. We knew nothing about caring for a handicapped child. And what kind of psychological scars had been left by the war and the death of their parents? Would the boys be able to adjust to America? We didn't have any Vietnamese friends in Washington who could help us bridge the gap between our cultures, and we didn't even know if we could cut through the red tape of adopting a handicapped refugee.

Besides, Debi and I were already overworked. We were both hoping to become partners in our respective law firms, and the stress from long hours and the pressure to succeed was taking its toll. Many of our peers were having marriage difficulties because of career demands, and I did not want to strain our own relationship by taking responsibility for raising two boys from another country.

Debi was undaunted by my objections. We had so much, and the refugees had so little. If we weren't ideal candidates for parenthood, who was? Our home would surely be better than no home at all, and anyway there was no way we could go back to life as usual after our experiences in the camp. Debi's arguments left me unconvinced, but I agreed at least to meet the boys on the following day.

The next morning, I drove into town with Chet, the Thai man working with our church. It seemed as if we were always running errands for something—plastic tubing for the deep water well, replacement parts for the camp's pub-

lic address amplifier, bamboo for a new classroom, note-
books and pens for the students. These simple chores were
time consuming and especially frustrating because we had
so little time left at the camp. As a tourist, bargaining for
souvenirs was often fun, but doing it every day for supplies
was maddening. I resented the long hours I had to spend
away from the refugees.

When Chet and I arrived back at camp, I was immediately
surrounded by a sea of waist-high children who were smiling
and laughing, and clinging to my knees. Some were making
fun of my bushy brown mustache by rubbing their fingers
across their upper lips and giggling. (Vietnamese men have
little facial hair, and most of the children had never seen
a man with a substantial mustache.) Others noticed my camera and began to beg me to take their picture. They framed
their eyes with their fingers, and then made clicking sounds
with their tongues. They laughed merrily as they snapped
their imaginary photos.

The press of tiny bodies was so strong against my legs
that I could not move for fear of stepping on unseen little
feet. There was no choice but to take a picture. The children
let out a spontaneous cheer as I focused the camera. One
picture did not satisfy them, and after taking a second one,
I was still unable to move away. My escape came only after
I knelt down and let each child touch my mustache. As
each little one came forward, there was a roar of delight
from the others, and one by one they ran home to tell
their families about their latest adventure with the American "giant."

As I walked toward the Children's Center, a man stopped
me in front of his barracks and in halting phrases asked
me to thank America for helping his people. Others around
him smiled and nodded, or bowed gently. I too bowed. A
woman from Debi's English class who was practicing her
newest vocabulary, greeted me with a majestic bow and
said, "Good morning, Mr. Debi." I responded with a bow.

While I was taking pictures at the Children's Center,
Debi nodded discreetly in the direction of Nhi and Hy. I
was startled by Nhi's appearance. His sharply curved spine
forced him to lean on his forearms to keep from falling

over. Thin trousers barely concealed his short, skeleton-like legs. He met my efforts to talk to him with an embarrassed smile, and a quick glance toward his brother for help.

"Hello, my name is Hy. This is my brother Nhi. What is your name?" Hy spoke haltingly, as if reciting the lines from a recently memorized English lesson.

I said my name slowly and carefully.

"Oh." The boy paused, as if wondering what to say next. "Very nice to meet you, Mr. Steve." I nodded, and returned to taking pictures of the other children. It had not been an overly promising encounter.

That evening, Debi and I went to visit Father Joe. He lived in a tiny single room furnished only with a cot, a desk, and a rusted metal folding chair. He had been at the camp since its opening two years earlier, and he was a tireless advocate for Vietnamese refugees. He rode his motorcycle to the camp every day carrying a large back pack full of supplies for the parentless children in the center. Even during mass, children hung on Father Joe's arms and he never sent them away. A legend among the refugees, he personified what someone once said of Dorothy Day: "She lived as if the Truth were really true."

Father Joe told us that he had been unable to find American parents for Nhi and Hy because of their age and Nhi's handicap. He spoke warmly of the boys and told us how devotedly Hy took care of his crippled brother. Nhi was well-liked by all the children in the center, and Hy was an outstanding student. "These two boys are among the finest kids I've ever met," concluded Father Joe. "If you decide to adopt them, I know you'll never regret it."

That night, before falling asleep, Debi and I talked for a long time about Nhi and Hy. I still had reservations, but the thought of becoming a father no longer seemed preposterous. Both these boys had so little; we had so much. How could we turn our backs and simply walk away from their problems? There were hundreds of thousands of refugees waiting to be processed through immigration, and we had been told several times that handicapped Vietnamese were seldom allowed into the United States. If we didn't adopt Nhi and Hy, it was likely that no one ever would. They could spend the rest of their lives in the camps or, if they were lucky, they might be sent to an orphanage.

Part of my reasoning was selfish. Debi and I were both afraid that when we returned to Washington we would fall back into the rut of our professional pursuits. Living with two Vietnamese boys would be a constant reminder of the needs of the world and our own need to keep an open heart. In the process of helping Nhi and Hy, we would also be helping ourselves.

Debi and I prayed together, and by the next morning we both felt an unusual peace about asking Nhi and Hy to become our sons. We waited until evening, until after the boys' soccer game, and then asked the boys to join us in Father Joe's office. We all sat on wooden benches and Nhi and Hy looked very solemn.

"Debi and I are going back to America," I said, speaking slowly and distinctly. "We want you to come live with us. You will be our sons, and we will be your parents. We hope you will say yes. If you agree, there will be five of us in our family—Debi, Steve, Loc, Nhi, and Hy. Do you have any questions?"

Hy turned to Nhi and did his best to translate. The boys talked together for several minutes in rapid Vietnamese, and then Hy asked in broken English, "Will you take my brother to the Capitol?" It seemed like a strange request, but we assured the boys that we would take them both to all the Washington monuments.

Hy shook his head and consulted again with Nhi. "No, no," he said. "I mean hospital. Will you take my brother there?"

Debi explained to the boys that Washington, D.C., had one of the best children's hospitals in the world. Nhi and Hy spoke together again, and we asked if they had more questions. Hy said yes, and then was silent. I thought he was feeling uneasy about making a decision, and I suggested that they take more time to think about it.

"No, no," Hy said quickly. "We will go."

That was it. Everything had happened with astonishing speed, but it seemed the most natural thing in the world that the four of us were now a family. Debi hugged Nhi and Hy and gave them a kiss, and I shook hands with both of them. Then the four of us walked to a party at the Children's Center, where Debi and I were the guests of honor at a going-away party. We were scheduled to leave for Washington the next morning, and Nhi and Hy would follow us when they were approved for immigration. The process might take months, and meanwhile Debi and I had many preparations to make for their arrival in America. Ahead of us lay a mountain of red tape that would baffle and challenge even the most determined of lawyers.

8
HY

A Strange Meeting

Our meeting with the two Americans in Father Joe's office was very strange. Even though Mr. Steve talked very slowly, I could not understand all his words. I thought he wanted to sponsor Nhi and me, but he held up five fingers and said, "Steve, Debi, Nhi, Hy" and "lock." Why was he speaking of a door latch? Then Mr. Steve explained he meant our Vietnamese teacher, Loc.* It is difficult for Americans to pronounce Vietnamese names.

I told Nhi that it would be great to go to Washington and live with Mr. Steve and Mrs. Debi. In the Vietnamese language, Washington is a very sophisticated word. Nhi and I talked about doctors for his legs and the need for a hospital. I was surprised when Mr. Steve said we would all go to the hospital, because I only wanted Nhi to go. Then I realized I had used the wrong word; "Capitol" and "hospital" sound almost the same to me. It is embarrassing that my English is so bad.

I wanted to make a good sentence, to tell Mr. Steve and Mrs. Debi, "Yes, we agree to come," but I could not find the right words. So I just said yes. I think that confused them. So I said yes again.

Then Mrs. Debi kissed me. It was the first time I was ever kissed by a woman. I did not know how to react. I felt like I was on a cloud. Mr. Steve shook my hand, and I felt very proud. In Vietnam I was too young to shake a man's hand.

The four of us went to a party at the Children's Center.

---

* Pronounced "Lop."

All our friends saw us walking with Mr. Steve and Mrs. Debi, and they wanted to know why we looked so happy together. I was afraid they would be jealous, but finally I told them we were going to be sponsored for the trip to America. The children congratulated us. I wondered if we really would be sponsored, or if Mr. Steve and Mrs. Debi would forget their promise when they were back home.

At the party, Mr. Steve and Mrs. Debi brought ice cream for all the children. Then they sang a song while Mr. Steve played the guitar. An older boy also sang a very sad song called, "Long Me" (The Heart of a Mother). The song spoke about how wonderful a mother is. She gives birth to her child and cares for the child as it grows. Her love is like the beginning of a waterfall at the top of a mountain. The water winds on a very long journey from the mountain to the ocean. The mother's love lasts forever like the waterfall, and is as great as the Pacific Ocean.

All the girls went outside and cried. I thought about my mother and wondered what she was doing. The love song reminded me of all the many things she had given us. I do not think I will ever find another person like her.

Two days later, we said good-bye to Mr. Steve and Mrs. Debi. Mr. Steve carried Nhi to the camp gate, and everyone stared at us. I always carried Nhi behind the barracks, even though it was harder to walk on the loose sand, so that everyone would not look at us. Now Nhi was very embarrassed, but Mr. Steve just smiled and nodded, and acted like he didn't care about the stares. As we neared the gate, a man sitting at a small restaurant said, "Thang que nay loi dung thang cha my." He meant Nhi was a leech to Mr. Steve, and that Mr. Steve was a low person because he carried a handicapped boy. Then the man laughed and said that Nhi makes love to his mother.

I looked at Nhi. He heard it too. The Vietnamese teachers walking beside us were pretending they did not understand. Mr. Steve turned and smiled at the cruel man. I felt so angry and embarrassed, but there was nothing I could do about it.

Mrs. Debi met us at the gate. She gave me an envelope, and Mr. Steve gave me a picture of Mrs. Debi. We said good-bye, and I carried Nhi back to the Children's Center. I did not turn around to look at Mr. Steve and Mrs. Debi; I knew we would probably never see them again.

"Hy, do you think they will sponsor us?" Nhi asked in a small voice.

"No," I answered. "It will be too difficult. Or maybe they will change their minds."

Nhi and I opened the envelope that Mrs. Debi gave us, and inside we found $10.00 worth of Thai money. So much money! We could have a party for our friends. I could buy a package of noodles for Nhi every evening.

I believed Mr. Steve and Mrs. Debi when they said they wanted to sponsor us—but not that strongly. Nhi and I hoped, and then we didn't hope. At night we talked about the Americans before we fell asleep and in the afternoon when I took my nap I looked at my picture of Mrs. Debi. She looked so beautiful. I missed her already, and it would be wonderful to have her for my American mother. Sometimes I showed the photograph to my friends. I wrote a letter, "Dear my adorable parents, Mr. Steve and Mrs. Debi." I asked them to send the sponsorship papers. But the papers never came.

When they had been gone a month, and still we had not heard from the immigration office, I decided to forget the Americans. Then one afternoon, as I was getting ready for a nap, I heard a voice reading over the loudspeaker a list of names of people who had been approved for immigration and would be leaving for Bangkok the next day. All of a sudden I heard, "Phan Van Nhi and Phan Van Hy, family of two."

The cook from the Children's Center ran over to see us. "It's you! You are sponsored. You are going to Bangkok tomorrow!" I did not understand. We had never been approved for immigration. Maybe it was a mistake. Or maybe the Americans had kept their promise. Only time would tell.

9
NHI

The Journey West

I was so surprised when Mr. Steve and Mrs. Debi said they wanted to sponsor us. I prayed every night to Buddha that they would keep their promise; if they didn't, we would probably spend the rest of our lives in the camp.

I was pretty sure the sponsorship wouldn't work out. The Americans would not like me because of my handicap. They would not want to take care of me the rest of my life, and I knew they said they would sponsor me only because they wanted to sponsor Hy. Sometimes I thought I should kill myself so that I would not be a burden to Hy anymore. It wouldn't make any difference if I got to America or not, because I would never be able to do anything important with my life. And maybe if I were dead, Mr. Steve and Mrs. Debi would feel so sorry for Hy that they really would adopt him.

We knew an adopted boy in Vietnam. When I was living with my mother in the small fishing village, the richest family in our town had a "con nuoi," a foster son. They adopted the boy because his parents died when he was only a small child, and they treated him like a servant. They beat him with sticks, just like they did their servants. Every day the boy walked past our house to take the family's five yellow cows and bulls to the field for grazing. Because he had to watch the animals in the hot sun all day, he never attended school. He was a "chan bo," a cowherd, which was one of the lowest jobs in Vietnam. It was a grave insult to call someone a "chan bo." If we did go to America, I wondered if we would be any better off than that poor chan bo.

I could hardly believe it when our names were called to go to Bangkok. We went by bus and spent the first day in a crowded, dirty refugee camp. There were many sick people and the water was not clean. Hy and I were nervous because the rules said sick people could not go to America.

With so many people, Hy could not carry me in a secret way like at the camp, and there was no place for me to go to the bathroom without people watching. It reminded me of the times I was away from home in Vietnam. Going to the bathroom on a squat toilet had been a daily nightmare, and I was always more afraid of going to the bathroom than of bullets. The war had come only once in awhile; the bathroom came every day. Only a person with crippled legs could understand my problem.

On the second day in Bangkok, a wonderful thing happened. A tall American named Mr. David came to the camp and said that we would be living with him at his house in Bangkok until we were approved to go to America. The house we drove to was beautiful—two stories, running water, fans, and a big yard. Three American children lived in the house, but when we tried to play together, we could not understand one another. Many people in the house asked Hy and me questions, and although we could not understand them, we always answered yes, because we wanted to be polite. I hoped they would not be angry with us because we did not talk more.

A woman in the house gave me an old wheelchair—a "car wheel" we called it in Vietnam. I could go outside and play with the other children without crawling in the dirt. She also gave Hy and me shoes. Usually, I could not wear sandals, because I did not have any muscles in my feet to keep them from falling off. But these shoes had strings to tie them to my feet. I felt very rich.

After a month at the house in Bangkok, Mr. David took us to the airport. The plane was so big and beautiful, and a stewardess was very nice. She asked us if we were hungry and brought us an American meal with a lot of meat. We ate, and then Hy slept while I looked out the window. I did not want to miss anything.

In Germany, we had to change planes. Hy carried me

on his back, and in the middle of the airport we came to
a sidewalk that was moving. Hy was afraid to get on, and
when he finally stepped forward, he almost fell. We had
seen escalators in the movies and heard about one in an
expensive hotel in Saigon. But we never knew there was
one that went straight across, instead of up and down.

In New York, a Vietnamese man met us at the plane
and took us on a huge bus. Hy tried to close the bus door,
but it wouldn't shut. The man told us to sit down, and then
the driver pushed a little handle, and the big door swung
closed. It was amazing.

As the bus drove through a big city, Hy and I talked to
each other excitedly. The streets were so clean; there was
no trash like on the sidewalks in Vietnam. And no one was
drying rice on the road, so the driver did not have to dodge
people. (When I was in Vietnam, I heard many people talk
about a wonderful American city called "Nuu Uoc." I didn't
learn until many months later after our ride through the
city that this *was* New York. I could not imagine how so
many people lived together in one place, and how they
walked up the many steps of tall skyscrapers like the Empire
"Straight" Building.)

On the bus, Hy and I asked our guide a lot of questions.
He was wearing a beige sport coat and looked very rich.
It made me worried when he said most Americans lived
in apartments because they could not afford a house. We
had stayed in an apartment when we first moved to Saigon,
and it was so poor and old and small—there wasn't even
a bathroom. I had not thought there would be such poor
living conditions in America. But our guide explained that
apartments in America were very nice.

We arrived at another airport, and our guide said good-
bye. Suddenly, Hy and I realized our bag was gone. "That's
it, he stole it!" I shouted. Hy and I felt very sad. We treated
that bag so carefully, because we had many things in it
which meant a lot to us—two pairs of pants, our treasure
of two tapes of Vietnamese music, and some important papers. I looked around for the guide, but he was gone.

Across the room, two doors opened and a group of people
went inside a tiny room. There were lighted numbers over

the doorway. The doors closed. When they opened again, the people were gone. I felt sick in my stomach. Would Hy and I have to go inside that room? Was this part of CIA technology? Perhaps we would disappear before we ever even saw Mr. Steve and Mrs. Debi.

Hy and I took our seats on the plane, and Hy fell asleep. Just then I saw a cart full of suitcases coming toward our plane. Our bag was on top! I tried to stay awake to see what New York looked like from the air; I wanted to look for many tall buildings, but as I looked and looked it took me to sleep. I slept all the way to Washington, until the stewardess woke us up. It was a disappointment; I wanted to see Washington from the air too.

As Hy carried me down the walkway, I wondered if Mr. Steve and Mrs. Debi and Loc would be there to greet us. Had the CIA told them the truth about our mother and father? What would happen to us if they didn't want us anymore? I didn't worry about Hy; he could take care of himself. But I needed someone to look out for me the rest of my life, and I did not want to be a beggar in the streets of America.

10
DEBI

"Your Children Are Not Your Children"

It was a quarter of seven on a cool September evening when we received word from New York that our new sons, Nhi and Hy, were arriving at Washington National Airport at 7:00 o'clock. With only fifteen minutes for a twenty-minute ride, Steve, Loc, and I ran down our front steps, pulling a wheelchair bumping along behind us.

All three of us were too excited and nervous to talk much during the ride. Steve concentrated on maneuvering through Friday evening rush hour traffic, while I tried to erase from my mind the image of two bewildered boys unable to speak English and lost in the weekend crowds of National Airport. After two months of legal efforts and all our careful planning, it was distressing to think Nhi and Hy would arrive from Vietnam without anyone to welcome them.

At the airport circle, traffic was bumper to bumper. Loc and I jumped out of the car, grabbed the wheelchair, and dodged honking taxis as we raced to the Eastern Airlines shuttle gate. Once inside, we heard the announcement that the boys' flight was a few minutes late. Steve ran up and squeezed my arm. "I told you we'd be early," he winked. It was 7:15.

As we waited for the boys, I noticed that Loc seemed to be at the edge of tears. "America is so rich, and Vietnam is so poor," he explained. "This airport reminds me of the great distance that separates our countries." Loc had been living with us since he had arrived in the United States one month earlier, and Steve and I were grateful that he would be available to act as interpreter and friend for Nhi and Hy.

Within a few minutes, a crowd of businessmen streamed from the shuttle gate. As the rush abated to a trickle, I finally caught a glimpse of the boys. Hy, deeply tanned and less than five feet tall, was wearing a plain white shirt and black pants. He made his way slowly up the ramp, carrying Nhi on his back. Nhi's arms were draped over his brother's shoulders, and his thin legs were wrapped around Hy's waist. For a brief moment, their frail figures and worried faces seemed to cast the specter of war across the cheerful, bustling room of the airport.

Steve and I gave the boys a big hug, as Loc helped Nhi into the wheelchair. The boys smiled timidly, but it was impossible to tell if they were smiles of bewilderment or happiness. We waited for their luggage, one small bag that held all their worldly possessions, and then we headed for home. The boys shivered in the cool night air.

Nhi and Hy were quiet during the ride to our new townhouse, which Steve and Loc and I had moved into only that day. We chose our new home because of its closeness to "Little Saigon" (a strip of Vietnamese stores and restaurants which was the center of the Vietnamese community in Arlington), and because the boys would be able to attend Arlington public schools, nationally known for their outstanding program for non-native-English-speaking students. On the way home, we pointed out Little Saigon to the boys, hoping the familiar names would help them feel more at home. It was the first time either boy had ridden in a car.

When we arrived home, the movers were busily arranging the furniture—in all the wrong rooms. Boxes and household appliances were spread over the floor. Despite the chaos, I felt overcome by joy. God had allowed me the privilege of becoming a mother to two war orphans, who had been without parents since the ages of seven and nine. My heart ached as I thought of how Nhi and Hy must have felt when their mother and father were killed. I looked forward to giving them the motherly love which they had suffered without for so long.

When our movers finally left, we joined hands and thanked God for Nhi's and Hy's safe arrival. Steve's parents and twin brother had stopped by to welcome the boys and offer moral support. I was grateful for the love and enthusiasm with which they joined our family circle. Steve brought out his guitar, and we sat in the living room, surrounded by boxes and singing "Michael Row the Boat Ashore." The words of this old spiritual took on new meaning as I thought of the many dangers Nhi and Hy had endured in their short lives.

As we were saying goodnight, Loc told us that Nhi and Hy had something important to tell us. "We lied about our ages," Hy said, looking very embarrassed. "Older men in the camps told us to reduce our ages so we could find a sponsor, but I am fourteen and Nhi is sixteen."

Steve and I were surprised that the boys were that old, although we had suspected from the beginning that the nine and thirteen years indicated on their papers was a fabrication. *Maybe it's a good thing we didn't know the truth*, I thought. The prospect of becoming a mother to teenagers might have scared me off. Now, there was no choice. I consoled myself with the thought that Vietnamese teenagers would be easier to cope with than their American counterparts. Since the boys had not grown up with us, it seemed unlikely that they would react against Steve and me in typical adolescent rebellion. Steve and I assured Nhi and Hy that their ages were irrelevant, and rejoiced with them that their long and dangerous journey was over.

At breakfast the next morning, Hy announced that he would not eat meat for two weeks to fulfill the promise he had made to Buddha during the flight from Vietnam. Steve and I hastened to assure him that we respected his decision, but I was reminded of the gulf which separated our religious beliefs. I hoped that Steve and I would find wisdom to make room for our sons' convictions without compromising our own commitment to following Christ. We had been warned by Father Joe that Nhi and Hy might pretend to convert to Christianity to please us, and we did not want to take advantage of the boys' vulnerability and dependence. Yet I found myself hoping that they would feel comfortable at Church of the Saviour, and join us in worship there.

In the afternoon, my parents stopped by to bring lunch,

and friends brought over bags of hand-me-down clothes. As we divided them between the boys, I handed Hy a wool sweater. "No, thank you, Mom," he protested. "I already have a sweater." His "sweater" was a thin sleeveless vest.

We spent the rest of the day unpacking, and then decided to splurge and take the boys to a fancy Vietnamese restaurant. After reading the menu, Loc seemed depressed—his thoughts turned to his father who was in a reeducation camp and hungry. Nhi and Hy, however, were jubilant. When a waitress asked Hy when he had come to America, he casually replied, "last night" and kept on eating. I admired the quiet dignity which both boys possessed, and wondered if they had noticed how many people in the restaurant were staring at us. I assumed the stares were an effort to make sense of our Vietnamese-American family. It was only months later that I learned the true reason for their strangely hostile attention—Nhi's handicap.

In the next few weeks, we quickly settled into a domestic pattern that made Steve and me, with our American notions, a bit uncomfortable. Politeness and respect for one's elders were deeply ingrained in Nhi and Hy—even when those elders were a young American couple struggling with instant parenthood. Each night they met us at the door when we returned home from work. They took our coats, handed us appetizers, and announced the gourmet results of several hours work in the kitchen. At dinner, they persistently resisted our efforts to get them to eat more food. Later, Hy explained the boys' dilemma: "We thought we should never eat more than you and Dad, and we were very sad to see how little you ate. Many times we went away hungry, and it was a long time before we understood that we could eat as much as we liked."

Steve and I repressed memories of returning home from work exhausted and snacking on junk food while TV dinners cooked. "You must not say thank you," our young chefs told us. "It is our duty." Delicious and relaxing as it was, we gently tried to discourage such elaborate treatment. Eventually, the boys took charge of weekday meals, while Steve and I covered the weekends—often with a highly regarded trip to McDonald's. Hamburgers, next to rice, were fast becoming the boys' favorite food.

One difficulty we were unprepared for was the resistance we met when trying to enroll Nhi in the English-as-a-second-language program. At the registration office, a school official informed me in a booming voice that handicapped, non-English-speaking students had to attend a high school on the other side of the county. Fortunately, I had taken a course in law school on the rights of the physically disabled, and after lengthy "negotiations" the official agreed to enroll Nhi—if the school could hire a teacher's aide to accompany him throughout the day. We did not want "special" education for Nhi; he would have enough trouble blending in and making friends without an adult hovering over him. We were extremely relieved when several days later, the school agreed to hire Loc as Nhi's permanent aide. Loc needed a job, he looked younger than he was, and he would appear to be just a student who had befriended Nhi. As Loc accompanied Nhi to school each day, our minister, Gordon Cosby, reminded us of a similar event in the life of Moses, whose own mother was hired to care for him by Pharaoh's daughter.

A week after getting Nhi into school, I was introduced at an Arlington County citizen's meeting as "the mother who took only two days to enroll her handicapped son in school." A murmur of approval went around the room. I realized for the first time that while I had been appalled by the obstacles placed in Nhi's path, his presence in the school represented a victory for handicapped children—and their parents.

Nhi's joy at attending school was soon tempered by a sobering trip to Washington's Children's Hospital. Before our first appointment, I explained to Nhi that he might be given braces and crutches, but there was a possibility that he would have to be content with a wheelchair. I told him about President Roosevelt, and assured him that he could have a good life "on wheels." Nhi was very quiet, and finally said faintly, "But I thought everyone in America could walk." It was the first hint we received that Nhi was expecting American doctors to give him back his legs.

. At the hospital, a doctor explained to Nhi that there was nothing anyone could do to restore his leg muscles. With months of difficult physical therapy, he *might* be able to walk short distances with the help of braces and crutches. The doctor cautioned us to consider carefully whether we even wanted Nhi to be fitted for braces. There was a strong possibility that he would never learn to walk, and falsely raised hopes and a failed effort could be devastating.

Back home, Steve and I, with assistance from Loc as interpreter, talked with Nhi about his options. We agreed that it was important for Nhi to try walking with braces, and if it did not work out, we would at least know that he had done his best. I would drive Nhi to physical therapy at Children's Hospital twice a week.

With the help of an outstanding physical therapist, Nhi made rapid progress. He had unusually strong arms, and despite his crooked back, within a month he was taking his first tentative steps on crutches. On Christmas day, he surprised us all by walking from our car to Steve's parents' house, a task which included climbing ten stairs. Steve and I agreed that Nhi's accomplishment and his new sense of self-confidence were among the best presents we had ever received.

By February, Nhi was traveling across town with Loc on the subway to get to Children's Hospital. In March, his physical therapist informed us he was ready to make the trip alone. When we gave Nhi the news, his eyes lit up. "I'm good enough to go by myself?" He was clearly thrilled, and Steve and he were able to override the objections which Hy and I expressed. "Don't worry, Mom, I'll be okay," Nhi said as he struggled out the door. "You do your work, and I'll see you at dinner tonight!"

At 3:30 I called Children's Hospital from my law office to see if Nhi had arrived. I breathed a silent prayer of thanks when the secretary informed me he was there. Later, I learned that Nhi had slipped in a puddle at Union Station, but two people had stopped to help him to his feet. Nhi was wet, but unhurt, and more determined than ever to make it by himself.

At 5:30 I called home to congratulate Nhi on his first solo round trip. When I learned that he was not yet home, I became alarmed. I called again at 6:00 and 6:30. No Nhi. I tried to hide the worry in my voice as each time Hy answered the phone.

At 7:30 Steve called to say that Nhi had finally made it home and that the three of them were eating dinner. Everything was fine and I could continue my efforts to meet a court deadline. It was only much later in the evening, when I called to say that I was on my way home, that I learned the truth. Nhi had taken a bad spill. He had caught a taxi from Children's Hospital to the subway station, and tried to go down the escalator instead of the elevator. A man rushing past him to meet a train had knocked his crutches out from underneath him. Nhi had fallen down the stairs, and did not remember anything until he woke up an hour later. He was lying on a bench, next to the subway, with his crutches beside him. His back and head hurt too much to move, but finally after several trains passed, he found the strength to get up and come home.

I hung up the phone crying. Steve had not taken Nhi to a doctor (Steve came from a family of five boys and he was not one to take physical bumps and blows too seriously), and I was angry that Nhi had not gotten medical attention. The thought of Nhi being knocked unconscious and lying unattended in the subway station left me weak. Surely many people had seen him fall; why hadn't there been one person who had called for help? As I rode home, it seemed to me that the whole world had become a cold, unfeeling place.

Nhi was asleep when I arrived, and I woke him up to check his eyes and see that his pupils were normal. His face was bruised, the side of his head was swollen, and his back was painfully strained. Otherwise, there seemed to be no serious damage.

"Mom," Nhi whispered sleepily, "I knew you would worry when I didn't come home, but when I was on the bench I couldn't get up. No one helped me; I don't understand why."

I was quiet for a moment as I tried to find a way to respond. How could I help Nhi understand when I didn't understand myself? "I don't know why either," I finally said. "I love you." I sat next to him until he fell asleep again.

I got up several more times that night to check Nhi's pupils and speech. I did not need an alarm clock to wake me; I slept fitfully, and thought often of Nhi lying uncared for in the subway station. Finally I wrote an anguished letter to a Washington newspaper, asking why so many evening commuters passed by my unconscious son.

In the morning, doctors examined Nhi and said there was no permanent damage, although it would be several weeks before he could attempt to walk again. Later in the week the newspaper published my letter and sent a photographer out to the house to take Nhi's picture. Nhi was excited to see himself in the paper, and we received many letters and telephone calls from people offering their help and sympathy. One woman, whose husband had recently died, volunteered to take Nhi to physical therapy. Another couple invited us to use their swimming pool—an offer we gratefully accepted. Everyone wanted to make sure we understood that there were still compassionate people left in our city.

A week later as I changed trains at Metro Center, the station where Nhi fell, I found myself wondering on which bench my son had lain. A woman with children who was standing near me leaned over to her husband and said, "This is where that poor little boy fell down the stairs last week. I can't believe no one helped him."

The woman's concern touched me. I thought about what a short time Nhi and Hy had been with us—only six months. Yet it was amazing how quickly "mother's guilt" had set in. I seldom worked evenings anymore, but I was at the office when Nhi fell. Could I have done more—should I have done more?

I realized now why it was so tempting for parents of handicapped children to coddle their kids. A little bit too much freedom, and their accidents could be severe, even fatal. A first solo subway ride would not hold such dangers for a child with two strong legs. But for Nhi. . . . He was all right now, but what about the future? What if he fell someday while crossing the street?

In the months that followed I gained the strength from family members and friends to let Nhi go. My mother-in-law continually quoted the words of Kahlil Gibran's *The Prophet,* "Your children are not your children."

"Children are human beings in their own right," Cathy Standiford explained. "They are created by God, and belong to God, not their parents. We are to love them, enjoy them, and watch them grow and mature. Then we must be prepared to say good-bye and launch them as God's creatures. We let them go, and if they are truly ours, they will come back. A handful of sand slips through the fingers if held tightly, but rests in our hand if we hold it loosely."

I learned similar lessons while waiting in doctors' offices or at physical therapy sessions with other mothers of handicapped children. Many of these women had watched their children suffer for years. One black woman, without a formal education, had raised a dozen foster and adopted children. She never gave advice or pep talks, but she radiated joy and strength as she shared her stories and listened to mine. I marveled that she had chosen again and again to voluntarily suffer with children—surely one of the most heartbreaking and emotionally draining jobs in the world. In her presence, I sensed that standing by children in their hour of need was an honor and a privilege.

During this time, occasionally someone asked me whether Nhi and Hy were becoming a strain on our marriage. I always answered with a resounding "No!" Our most difficult year of marriage was the one before we went to the refugee camp. We worked long hours, worried about pleasing our superiors, and then came home with two deflated egos. Neither of us had anything left with which to pump up the other. Now we were both rejuvenated by the time we spent together as a family. Our pillow talk was about our joint parenting.

Most wonderful of all, I found myself falling in love with Steve all over again. Our love had the same freshness and newness that it did when we were dating, when I was just getting to know him and was delighted to discover all his wonderful qualities. Nhi and Hy needed Steve in ways that I did not. As I watched him carry Nhi, teach the boys basketball and the art of dipping French fries into catsup, and as I listened to his prayers for them, I knew I was getting to know my husband better than if our family had not suddenly doubled.

11
STEVE

Rice 1,460 Times a Year!

Sweat ran down my face and neck, and soaked my cotton flannel shirt as I climbed up the mountain carrying Nhi on my back. We were in the middle of the Appalachian mountain range, heading up Humpback Rock, with Debi and Hy close behind us. I had made this steep climb many times before, but never with a seventy-pound boy on my back. We were only halfway up, and already I wanted to turn back, but my pride wouldn't let me. Debi had said it couldn't be done, and Nhi had offered to wait in the car until the rest of us returned. Their protests made me all the more determined; I wanted to include Nhi in all our family activities, and I assured him that there would be no problem carrying him to the top.

"Dad, are you heavy?" Nhi whispered anxiously in my ear.

"Only a little," I replied softly, touched by his concern, and not wanting Debi to hear.

"Oh, Dad, you are so strong!" Nhi whispered in a tone of admiration, massaging my shoulders—and my ego. With this encouragement, I quickened my pace. After an hour of climbing, including many rest stops, we reached the top. College students and other hikers basked in the warm October sun on top of the huge bare slab of rock that jutted out into the sky. I found a safe place for Nhi to sit, and the four of us looked out at a remarkable landscape.

At our feet, the trees formed a majestic, variegated carpet of fall colors that stretched for miles down the mountains into the Shenandoah Valley. Hawks with outstretched wings hovered effortlessly above us in the cloudless sky. In the

distance, fields, farm houses, white wooden fences, and grazing cattle completed the pastoral scene.

Worn out by the hike, but pleased by my accomplishment, I removed my sweat-soaked shirt to cool off. I noticed
Hy staring at my chest. He turned to Debi, and in an almost
reverential voice, said, "Mom, now I see why Dad is so
strong. Even the strongest men in my country do not have
a mustache on their chests."

I looked at Debi smugly. She rolled her eyes in response.
It seemed to me that there was a lot to be said for having
two admiring teenage sons.

Sitting there on top of the world, I felt a deep sense of
peace about our new family of four. The fears and anxieties
that plagued me at the refugee camp were gone. In their
place was the same deep sense of usefulness and purpose
I had experienced while working with the refugees in Thailand, a contented euphoria that members of our mission
group still referred to as the "Songkhla high." So far, being
a father to Nhi and Hy had been a lot like climbing up
Humpback Rock—hard work, but exhilarating. I was
amazed that I had so much energy to meet the demands
of work and family life. It was as if by responding to the
needs of Nhi and Hy, Debi and I were being blessed by a
deeper capacity to love. I was sure that the "high" we were
experiencing as a new family would soon be followed by
a more normal domestic routine—including the ups and
downs of daily living, but for the time being I intended
to enjoy the honeymoon.

As the months went on, it seemed the honeymoon would
never end. There were minor setbacks like Debi's difficulty
enrolling Nhi in high school, and his subway fall, but the
burden I anticipated in caring for two orphans never materi-
alized. Nhi and Hy were a joy to be with—cheerful, inquisi-
tive, and always eager to learn. Their cherubic smiles and
gentle manner soon won the hearts of all of our friends
and most of our family. Hy was a bundle of energy, and
practiced his English with everyone he met. He greeted
each new acquaintance with a slight bow and handshake,
and although he often had to stop in mid-sentence to search
for words, he was communicative and outgoing. At school,

Hy was a model student—courteous, studious, hard-working, and teachable. Nhi, whose English was still limited, was more reticent about speaking. Although he always smiled when spoken to and said "nice to meet you," he understood little of the conversations that followed. He limited his own communication to one-word answers, and never asked anyone to repeat a question. Instead, he smiled and nodded pleasantly. There were times when I wondered if we would ever really get to know Nhi.

Debi reveled in her new role of being a mother. Her law firm allowed her to work half time in order to spend more time with the boys, and she dutifully arranged for medical and dental examinations, enrolled the boys in the local high school, bought rice, chopsticks, and an Oriental cookbook, and attended to a hundred other errands. At times I thought she was pushing the limits of mothering— tucking Nhi and Hy into bed and giving them a good night kiss before they went to sleep. It was a part of my wife I had not seen before, and the contrast to our lives as upwardly mobile workaholic lawyers was striking.

One of the most exciting aspects of our new lives was introducing Nhi and Hy to the wonders of American technological society. They were astonished that they would live in a home with a telephone, and they spoke admiringly of our stove, refrigerator, dishwasher, stereo, and tape deck. Their home in Vietnam was without modern plumbing, and for several weeks showers and baths were a special delight. It was not long, however, before they began to take the wonders of their new world for granted. A few weeks after their arrival, we visited my parents, and Hy and Nhi asked their new grandmother where she kept her microwave oven. They were disappointed to learn that not all Americans owned this convenient but expensive appliance.

On our first visit to the supermarket, both boys were overwhelmed by the abundance of food. Nhi, who was enjoying the new freedom provided by his wheelchair, rode up and down the aisles, gazing in admiration at the well-stocked shelves. The limited options of the open-air market in Vietnam, as well as the years in which the boys had lived without adequate food, made our local grocery store seem like a fantasy world. When we got to the check-out counter, Hy was disturbed that I paid the bill without an argument. "Dad, aren't you going to bargain to get the best price?" Remembering my experiences in the Thai marketplace, I was grateful for the inflexibility of pre-marked prices.

It was food which forced Debi and me to make one of our most major adjustments to the presence of our new sons. For the first few months, we were awakened every morning by the smell of frying fish and the pungent aroma of "nuoc mam"—fish sauce. The sauce, which we learned to love (for dinner), was made by percolating water through layers of decomposing squid and salt. It was months before Nhi and Hy learned to like Wheaties and Cheerios for breakfast, and Debi and I felt especially sacrificial as we suffered silently through numerous bouts of "morning sickness."

We had learned in Thailand that Vietnamese people eat a lot of rice, and to help Nhi and Hy feel at home, Debi and I decided that we would fix rice every evening. But we were unprepared for the boys' definition of "a lot"— each and every meal, including breakfast, plus an afternoon snack. That was rice 28 times a week, or 1,460 times a year. I thought I would learn to like a daily serving, but after a few weeks, I was unable to eat anymore. The boys never grew tired of rice, and we began to purchase it in 25-pound bags from a local Vietnamese store.

At every meal, Nhi and Hy participated in an elaborate, sometimes frustrating ritual, in which they offered choice pieces of food from their plates to Debi and me. It was a sacrificial gesture from a society where food was scarce and many people left their family table hungry. To forego a part of a meal so that others might eat was a daily occurrence in Vietnam, and Nhi and Hy were astonished to learn that we considered it impolite to force food from our own plates onto the plates of others. It was many weeks before they gave up offering us food, and a good portion of our mealtime was consumed by our effort to explain American table manners.

By far the biggest adjustment for all of us was communication—the lack of it. Nhi and Hy spoke only a few English words, and with Loc gone most evenings to a local community college, Debi and I were often on our own. With the help of our English-Vietnamese dictionaries and awkward pantomimes, the four of us understood each other some of the time. Vietnamese, we discovered, was a tonal language, and a single word could have six different meanings, depending on its pronunciation. "Ba" for instance, might mean father, uncle, trash, grandmother, she, or the number three. Said twice it was the brand name of a popular French beer sold in Saigon—"33."

It was soon obvious that the only way the four of us could live together was if Nhi and Hy learned English—quickly. Fortunately, their high school English-as-a-second-language program was outstanding, and for six hours every day, Nhi and Hy were drilled by dedicated teachers in vocabulary, phonics, grammar, pronunciation, reading, writing, and idioms. Instead of regular math and science courses, they were instructed in "The Language of Math" and "The Language of Science." Here, they learned words like "equation," "plane," "triangle," and "graph" which would prepare them for advanced academic studies.

Nhi's and Hy's fellow students were a stimulating group of Vietnamese, Ethiopian, Afghan, Chinese, Cambodian, and Central American teenagers. They were almost all hardworking students, some of whom went to high school at great hardship to their families. Most of these families did not speak English, and after a few weeks, it became apparent that Nhi and Hy were at a distinct advantage because they returned home to English-speaking parents. Informal "classes" continued at the dinner table in the evenings and on weekends.

Although there were occasional frustrations, the results of Nhi's and Hy's total immersion in English was dramatic. Both become outstanding students in their classes, and our friends at church marveled at their rapid progress. One night a few months after their arrival, I checked on Nhi and Hy while they slept only to discover that Hy was speaking English in his sleep.

In the process of helping Nhi and Hy with English, we

discovered some of the serious difficulties in our native language. One evening, while Nhi was studying idioms, he explained to me the many uses of "call." To call *up* means to telephone, while to call *down* means to reprimand. To call *on* is to select but to call *off* is to cancel. To call *in* means to report, although you call *out* the National Guard. I began to appreciate afresh the difficulties my sons faced.

During study breaks and on weekends, I enjoyed introducing Nhi and Hy to American sports. They were familiar only with soccer, and they laughed heartily when I explained to them about basketball, a game played with the hands. Nonetheless, we were soon playing regularly together on a nearby public court, and they both learned to dribble, pass, and shoot with some amount of skill. They also learned vital street slang and how to exchange high five handshakes to celebrate an "awesome" move on the basketball court.

By mid-winter, Nhi and Hy were both avid fans of the University of Virginia basketball team, and an oversized picture of 7'4" Ralph Sampson covered the front of our refrigerator. Nhi, who had trouble remembering American names, referred to Sampson as "the tallest man," and we spent our Saturday afternoons glued to the television.

Near the end of March, Nhi and Hy went to school one day with a note from me which read, "Please excuse Nhi and Hy Phan from classes today for a family outing." We headed straight for a nearby sports arena and bought three tickets from a scalper to watch the first round of the Atlantic Coast Conference Basketball Tournament. Our seats were perfect—center court, seven rows up, and eye level with "the tallest man." We gorged ourselves on hot dogs, peanuts, popcorn, and ice-cold Cokes, and shouted enthusiastically as we watched Virginia handily dispose of an outclassed Georgia Tech team. I looked over at Nhi and Hy, and thought back to my own teenage years. Playing hooky had never felt so good.

12
HY

At Home in "The Beautiful Country"

I always told myself that if I ever got to America, I would kiss the ground first thing. But when Nhi and I finally arrived in Washington, D.C., there was no ground, only concrete. It was just one of many surprises that have come our way in the six months we have been in the United States.

My first impressions left me startled and afraid. At the airport Nhi and I were forced to pass under a machine that I assumed to be a gold detector. A man in a uniform checked our bags very carefully and then traced our bodies with a long metal stick. I was glad we had no gold, and I wondered if the pirates we met in the Gulf of Thailand knew about the technology they were missing.

Everyone around us looked so civilized with their suits and beautiful dresses. All the women had smooth shiny legs, but I did not understand how their legs could be a different color from their arms and faces. I was even more puzzled by the public drinking fountain. It was a silver metal box attached to the wall, and a man was holding his son up to take a drink. The boy turned a knob on the side of the box, and a stream of water immediately sprang forward. The boy drank a little, but the rest of the water disappeared back into the box. Several other people followed him and drank from the same box. I couldn't believe that a country as rich as the United States could recycle water; such a dirty way to drink, I thought, must make many people sick. We had cleaner water in Vietnam.

We walked out of the airport with Mr. Steve and Mrs. Debi, and even though it was night, there were so many lights, it wasn't dark. I was disappointed by the looks of the car that Mr. Steve drove. It was old and rusty, not big and black as I had imagined. Still I was excited to have my first car ride. As we drove down the streets I noticed that there were no people on the sidewalks. *This is America!* I thought. *I have come to "the beautiful country," just like my friends who left Vietnam before me, and here everyone has a car. No wonder there is no one walking!*

When we arrived at our new house, everything was a mess. There were men carrying furniture in and out, and there were boxes all over the floor. It was hard to tell whether our new American parents were very rich—or poor. The house was big and modern, with three stories. And there were an unusual number of machines to do all the work, to wash the clothes and dishes, to suck dirt off the floor and cook the food in a few seconds. But our new mother and father drove an old car and I did not see any servants. It was hard to understand.

That first night, Mr. Steve's brother brought us a big piece of meat covered with red sauce wedged between two pieces of white bread. It was delicious. "McDonald's," the brother said. I admired how quickly the meal was prepared.

Mr. Steve's parents shook our hands, and his father asked me how old I was. "Nine," I replied.

"You are big for nine," he remarked, and I felt afraid.

When we were getting ready for bed (without mosquito nets!), Loc came into the room and asked us to tell him our true ages. We told him our papers were wrong; we were really fourteen and sixteen. Loc advised us to tell Mr. Steve and Mrs. Debi right away. I was afraid that we would be kicked out of the house for lying, and I wondered where we would go and how we would feed ourselves.

But I was so surprised. Mr. Steve and Mrs. Debi were not angry. They said they would help us fix our papers, and asked us to call them "Mom" and "Dad." I tried the words. They sounded funny, but somehow I felt exuberant. I slept well.

Two days after we arrived, Mom and Dad took us to their church. They said we did not have to go, but I was afraid they would be angry if we stayed at home. I hated Christians, and I did not want to take part in their worship service. It made me angry that there were people who did not believe in Buddha, and I thought the people at the church would hate me because I was a Buddhist and not like them.

The church was a strange place. The Christians there welcomed me warmly and spoke kindly. Many of them gave me hugs and kisses. I even saw white people hug black people, as if they were friends. In Vietnam the communists told us that Americans hate black people a great deal, and hate Vietnamese only a little less. It was hard to know what was true.

At the end of every prayer, all the people said "Amen." It is the word that Vietnamese Catholics who don't love Buddha use. I am in a new country and many things I do are new, but there are some things that must never be given up. I will never say that word "Amen."

After church, we drove around the city. Nhi and I laughed at the fat birds in Washington that people called "pigeons." In Vietnam, they would have been eaten long before they became so plump. We drove through tunnels much bigger than the ones we hid in during the war, and then something frightening happened. Mom and Dad parked the car, and started walking through a field of tall grass. I couldn't believe that they could be so careless. I forced myself to follow, but I thought at any moment I would hear an explosion. I looked carefully before I put down each foot; a land mine could be anywhere. I did not want to become like a school friend who had blown himself to pieces just because of one careless step.

A few days later, Nhi and I started school. A Vietnamese man interviewed us, and I was ashamed to see that he wore a brown jacket with large yellow patches on each elbow. To wear mended clothes in America! In Vietnam, I always hated rich people, because they took money from the poor. But in America, I thought it was better that people think my family was rich. When people asked me questions about my Vietnamese parents, I always described my rich relative's house. I told them that in Vietnam we had a real bathroom and three floors, and that my parents were schoolteachers. It was important that people love and respect us.

After our interview, Nhi and I went to classes for students still learning to speak English. I was amazed when the teacher gave me a textbook written exactly for my grade. In Vietnam, I only knew about two kinds of books, one for adults and one for children. I wondered what technology enabled people to write so precisely.

School was very interesting to me, but sometimes I was lonely. In Vietnam everyone knew me, and I often led my friends in sports and other adventures. In America, no one even said hello to me. Everyone already had a lot of friends. They didn't need a new one. It was even worse when I made a mistake in front of a girl. A classmate asked me for help on a problem. I told her there were twenty-six hours in a day. I was so embarrassed.

For the first few weeks of school, Mom made us lunch. It was a thick brown paste and a sweet red syrup between two pieces of brown bread. Nhi said it was the same kind of brown spread the Americans gave him in the orphanage. I was surprised to learn it was made from peanuts, but I was more surprised to learn that our new parents ate brown bread. In Vietnam, only poor people buy brown bread. The rich eat soft white bread. Anyway, I poured soy sauce all over my sandwiches to make them taste better.

I like my new mother and father, but it makes me uncomfortable to see how strangely they treat one another. Sometimes Mom tells Dad what to do. Dad lets her drive the car. And once I even saw Mom beckon to Dad with her palm up, the way we call animals in Vietnam. I was surprised that Dad did not get angry. It makes me angry when my new mother does not treat me with the respect due an older son. She asks me to do chores, but she has no right to speak to an older son in this way. It is something I will have to get used to, but it is very hard.

The strangest American custom I have encountered is kissing. The first time I encountered this was in the refugee camp, when Dad kissed Mom on the lips shamelessly in front of my friends and me. Vietnamese tradition dictates that kissing in public is inappropriate, and I was very embarrassed. Besides, Vietnamese do not kiss on the lips. They smell the cheek as if to say they accept the skin odor, be it fragrant or otherwise. Lip kissing seemed to say that the lovers accepted each other's saliva, be it free of germs or not. The more I thought about this, the more I admired the risky Americans.

It was such a new experience at the time, I was unaware that it was only the first of several surprises and lessons kissing was waiting to offer me. I received many kisses when I first arrived in America, and on my first day of school I almost walked into another schoolmate as I stared at two students who were kissing each other in the hall. They twisted and turned their heads while kissing fervently. It seemed as if they were trying to extract something precious hidden somewhere in the other person's mouth. The way these lovers worked their lips reminded me so much of the fighting fish I used to own in Vietnam. When put into a jar filled with water, two fighting fish would bite and hang onto each other's mouth while trying to push the opponent into a corner. The weaker fish would try to yank its mouth away and swim for its life. During most of the fight, the fish pressed on each other's mouths, just as the lovers pressed on each other's lips. Happily, I saw that the lovers' lips did not come out bruised like my fishes' mouths.

After that first day, I noticed that American boyfriends and girlfriends almost always kissed each other during the change of classes. Though knowing that they would be apart for an hour at most, many of them still refused to give up kissing. I concluded that Americans enjoy being repetitious.

With so many new things to learn and experience, our first semester of American school went by very quickly. Soon it was Christmas. Nhi and I received many wonderful presents from our new parents and grandparents, and I even got a watch. I put it in my pocket when we went outside so that no one would tear it off my wrist. Looking at all my presents at first made me happy, but then I felt sad. I thought about my mother and father in Vietnam, and my brother and sister. I wondered what they were doing, and if they would ever be able to share in our happiness in America.

I am very afraid that our American Mom and Dad will find out we lied to them and that our parents are still living. There have already been many close escapes. I learned that Granddad works for the CIA, and I worry all the time that our family will show up in his computers. Then we were at a dinner party, and Mom and Dad introduced us to an American general who had stayed in Quang Ngai, a town where my family lived for several years. I never dreamed I would meet such a big man; it was like facing a powerful tiger or a dragon. The general asked me about my family, and when I told him my father was a doctor killed in the town of Mo Duc, he was surprised. "I never heard of a doctor killed in Mo Duc," he said. Then he told me that he would like to talk with me again. I was feeling very nervous and tried to stay away from the general for the rest of the evening.

After that Nhi and I were more careful than ever. Mom and Dad encouraged us to talk in Vietnamese with one another in our bedroom (we used English at the dinner table, so that Nhi and I would learn to speak it quickly), but we seldom followed this suggestion. Our American parents said that they did not know how to speak Vietnamese, but how could we be sure that they were telling the truth? Perhaps they had secret tape recorders in our room, and that is why they wanted us to speak freely. I worried too that they might be able to read Vietnamese, or that they would have our letters from home translated. Whenever the mailman came, I always hurried to see if there was a letter from Ma. Then I quickly hid it, and Nhi and I only read it when we were alone.

The secret of our parents was a heavy burden about my neck, and I often wished that we could talk to Mom and Dad about it. But I had to think about Nhi. The American doctors said they could not fix his legs, and I was not old enough to take care of him all by myself. I promised Ma and Ba in Vietnam that I would always look out for Nhi, and even though our lives were different now, Nhi was still my responsibility. Our new Mom and Dad say that he must learn to take care of himself, and even do his own laundry, but I know this cannot happen. Nhi will never walk. It is my duty as his brother to take care of him, and I will never tell my American parents about my Vietnamese parents until I am able to take care of Nhi—for the rest of our lives.

13
NHI

Troubles and Triumph

It is the last day of my first year in American high school, and I am walking with friends to an awards assembly. I never had friends before, and I never walked before. Now with the help of my braces and crutches, I can go wherever I want. Or at least most of the time. I don't really want to go to this assembly, but even with braces and crutches, there are still things I have to do.

So much has changed since I first came to this school. During my first weeks of class, I was lonely and embarrassed. All the children in my class spoke different languages, and when the teacher asked a question in English, there would be a flood of whispers in Spanish, Vietnamese, Laotian, Farsi, Afghani, and other languages. I did not understand anything, not even when the teacher asked me my name. Another Vietnamese student translated for me, and I could see the beautiful Spanish girls on the other side of the class giggling and talking together. I knew they were talking about me.

At lunch time, Loc, who was my teacher's aide, pushed me into the cafeteria where there were hundreds of boys and girls crowded together. He left me at an empty table near the wall, and went to buy his lunch. It seemed like he was gone for an hour. At first I sat motionless, frozen with fear, and then I turned my wheelchair around so I faced the wall.

I loved the peanut butter and jelly sandwiches that Mom made for me, but I could hardly bite off a piece and chew it. I hunched over my sandwich, and hoped my neck, shoulders, and arms were like a wall that hid me from the view of other boys and girls. I knew there were a thousand people looking at me. My stomach churned as I thought of them pointing at me and making jokes about my crippled legs.

I wished my wheelchair would disappear. "Oh Buddha," I prayed. "I wish I could get up and walk to a table like everyone else and say this wheelchair is not mine." But it was mine, and now it was not only my legs that were paralyzed, but my whole body, and my mind. The lunch hour seemed to last forever. I looked out a window and saw leaves falling from a tree. It was a gloomy day, and I thought sadly of my family in Saigon. My parents and younger brother and sister would be huddled together in our small house watching the rain come down, and thinking of the ones who were lost to America.

When Loc pushed me down the hall in my wheelchair, I stared at the floor and sat still as a statue. I knew that people would be staring at me as we passed by, and although I could not understand any English, I was certain they must be talking about me and laughing. My only comfort was that I had nice clothes. Maybe other students would think that, with Loc to push me, I was a very rich person. Then they might want to get to know me.

As the weeks went by, I started to feel less strange and awkward. American students did not tease me or laugh at my legs as I thought they would. Instead, they came up to me and tried to become friends. The Vietnamese students in my classes still treated me like I was stupid, just like in Vietnam, and I was not friends with them. But I made other friends in the class. My three best friends were from Afghanistan, Turkey, and Czechoslovakia.

Making friends was not my biggest surprise. I started to make good grades in English classes. I always heard people say that polio had attacked my brain and made me stupid, and I never studied hard because I knew it was useless. Now I started wondering if maybe I was smart.

One of the only problems I had during this time was food. In the refugee camp, we learned that Americans eat six times a day, and I was looking forward to always being full. But my first two months in America, I never got enough to eat. Hy and I thought we shouldn't eat more than Mom and Dad, and they ate so little. In Vietnam we were not permitted to help ourselves to food, and we depended upon others offering it to us. But even though Mom and Dad offered us more food, if we said no, they did not offer again. In Vietnam, it is impolite to say yes to the first offer of food. It must be offered several times by the parents before the child finally accepts.

It was a long time before I learned that we could help ourselves to food and accept it the first time it was offered. But then the food was so tasteless. Sometimes when I wanted to add salt or fish sauce, or soy sauce, they were on the other side of the table, and I could not think of the English words needed to get them.

Table manners were another problem. In Vietnam, children wait for parents to eat, and parents wait for grandparents. In America, sometimes the mother tells the family to start eating while she is still at the stove. Then instead of putting the serving bowl in the middle where everyone can reach it, it is passed around. Food on the plates cannot be mixed all together, and instead of using chopsticks and bringing the bowl up to your chin, we have to leave the plate on the table and balance food on forks to bring it to our mouths. We can't suck meat bones clean, and we have to chew with our mouths shut.

The thing I miss most about eating is the Vietnamese ritual of sharing food and love during a meal. Because food was scarce, everyone always erred on the side of taking less than his share. We took a big portion of rice and only a small piece of fish. Then each family member offered some of his or her food to other members of the family, and no matter how much that person wanted or needed the food, he always declined. Then the giver offered again and again until the person finally accepted. All of us were hungry, and we almost always left the table hungry, but for my first sixteen years, we shared this spiritual kinship of sacrifice and giving whenever we sat down to eat.

Meals lost their meaning in America. Since we no longer lived on the edge of existence, we no longer had the deep need to share our food each day. We did not think about the deep meaning or value of food. When we tried to give our food to Mom and Dad, they declined, but when we offered it again and again, they still declined. Finally, we learned it was not polite to eat off someone else's plate.

The strangest part of my life in America is knowing that my parents are still in Vietnam. There are times like when we went to Humpback Rock and saw the magnificent fall colors, and my American dad was carrying me on his back, that I feel like I am a part of a new family. I know that Mom and Dad love me very much, and the lie that is between us is like a dark, heavy thing inside me. I try to forget about the lie, but it comes up every day, every minute, every second.

One time Mom and I were talking about babies. She asked me if I ever played with my aunt's and uncle's babies. I had to think fast. Half of me tried to figure out, was my youngest cousin too old for me to say "yes"? Did I live in Saigon when he was a baby? The other half of me started thinking sadly about my younger brother who was still in Vietnam. *Yes, yes, of course,* I thought. *I played with him every day, and I loved taking care of him. I love babies!* I wanted so much to tell Mom about him. But I knew that was impossible. Just a simple question, and suddenly I had to decide whether to lie again. "Ah, no Mom, I never played with babies," I said, not looking at her face. What if someday she guessed I was lying?

Every time Hy or I told Mom or Dad a lie, as soon as we were free, we would tell one another what we said so that our stories would be the same. This system worked well for a while, but gradually we forgot to keep one another up to date.

Hy was especially burdened by the lie, and sometimes after a letter from Vietnam or when our American parents showed us how much they loved us, he would say, "I'm going to tell Mom and Dad everything; it would be better for them to know about us."

Then I would say, "Oh, come on, Hy. You don't want to do that. We'd really be in trouble then."

Sometimes Hy persisted. "But I must tell them," he would say.

"You know they will kick us out if you do, and we won't

have a place to stay," I argued. This usually stopped Hy, and in a few minutes he would change his mind. At least for awhile our secret was safe.

There were times when I wanted to tell Mom and Dad the truth, too, but if they kicked us out, my worst fear would come true. Sometimes I had vivid nightmares in which Hy and I were forced to go back to Vietnam. I saw our house in Saigon just as it was when we left. A dim fluorescent light hung in the front room. When we got to the house, suddenly I had no wheelchair or crutches, and I was crawling on the ground. No one knew that I was a good student in school. The dreams seemed so real, and Ma and Ba were ashamed before our neighbors that we had been forced to return to Vietnam.

Hy and I were terrified when Dad said to us several times that he thought it was strange that we had nine cousins in the West, but did not know any of their addresses. This was the one part of our story that was true, even if it was hard to believe. Hy and I did not know what to say, because we did not want to draw attention to our other lies.

Sometimes it seems to me that life is very unfair. For seventeen years, my life has been messed up. First the war and being handicapped, then being poor under the communists. Now when life is finally good and we should all be happy together, there is this terrible lie. Mom and Dad would be so hurt and angry if they found out we lied. They treat us like their own sons, so all I can do is try as hard as I can to forget that I have a family in Vietnam, and try in every way to please my new mom and dad.

It isn't always easy to please an American mother and father. One morning Dad was irritated when he saw me wearing the same cowboy shirt for the fourth day in a row. He spoke quickly in English to Mom, and I felt that I had not pleased them, but I did not know what I had done. Mom went to get me a clean shirt. It was so different than in Vietnam, where I only had one shirt for school. I wore the same shirt for seven consecutive days without washing it. Everyone did. My other clothes were ragged and yellowed with wear, hand-me-downs from neighbors.

Another time, Hy and I wanted to make Mom happy

when she came home from work. So we hid under the coffee table and in the closet. When Mom came inside, we jumped out and said "Hu!" In Vietnam, parents always play that game with their children, and they act very scared. Then the children and parents laugh together. But Mom jumped and said we should never do that again. We felt so stupid that we had made her afraid instead of making her laugh.

One thing that made me angry about my new mother and father is that I had to do chores in the house. In Vietnam, everyone knew that I was too handicapped to work, so they took care of me. I thought that when I came to America and lived with a rich family that they would have servants. I wouldn't have to do anything. But here Dad bragged to his friends that we all did the housework together. He told them that I cleaned the bathrooms, and it always made me so angry and embarrassed. But I did not tell Mom and Dad how I felt, because I was afraid to speak of my bad thoughts.

During this time, the American doctors told me that they could not fix my legs. My dream of playing soccer and running like Hy was broken. My parents had spent all their money so that I could leave Vietnam and find American doctors, who we all thought could fix anyone. When the doctors first told me my legs were hopeless, I felt discouraged. But I still kept a little hope. I remembered that people in the refugee camp said that German doctors were better than American doctors at helping handicapped people. I thought that one day when I was older I might go to Germany, and maybe the doctors there would help me walk.

Although the American doctors said they couldn't fix my legs, they said they could fix my back. This made me very happy. My back used to be straight, but every year it becomes more and more crooked. I worry that it will bend so far that it will just break. It looks pretty weird. And it has become so painful. I can only sit on one hip, and I have to hold myself up with one arm or I will fall over. I used to lie down a lot in Vietnam, but going to school I sit up all day, and my back hurts all the time. It is wonderful to think that doctors can take away this pain.

Meanwhile, the doctors have given me braces and crutches. They said I might be able to walk with them, but they weren't sure. At first I didn't like using them; it was too hard and my legs were too little. I was so afraid of falling. But after months of physical therapy, I got used to walking, and I was so excited when Mom and Dad let me go places on my own.

My first subway ride was a disaster. All I remember is falling, and then I was unconscious. When I woke up, I was all alone and lying on a bench. I was sad to think that no one helped me. But I remembered in Vietnam people said that failure is the mother of success. So that encouraged me, and when my pain went away, I started walking again.

That is why today I am walking to a school assembly with friends. Mrs. Bratt, the Chairman of the English-as-a-second-language classes told me to sit in the middle chairs in the front of the room because I am going to receive an award. I will have to walk to the front of the gym with everyone watching, and shake hands with the principal. I wonder how I will keep from falling down. I haven't learned yet how to shake hands while I'm on crutches. I need both hands to keep from falling.

I hope people will not laugh at me because I look so strange. And I wonder what kind of award I am going to get. I have never been good at anything before; it is something new that people think that I should receive an award.

14
DEBI

Bedside Vigil

Steve and I slipped in the back door of the high school
gymnasium and quickly found a seat with a group of other
parents. Earlier in the week we had received a call from
Terry Bratt, the chairperson of Nhi's program, informing
us that Nhi would receive her department's award for "best
student." Steve and I were invited to join the other parents
whose children were also being honored at the awards assembly.

Now Steve and I sat apprehensively as each department
chairman announced its winner, and the students went forward to receive their awards. Most of the students sitting
in the bleachers seemed bored with the whole procedure.
Many of them talked with their friends and a few clapped
politely when the winners were announced.

I spotted Nhi sitting among other teenagers waiting for
awards. What will be the reaction of these students when
my son awkwardly walks forward on his braces and
crutches? Will they laugh? And how will Nhi feel if he hears
them making fun of him?

My heartbeat quickened when I saw Terry Bratt walk
to the podium. "This year's outstanding student is Nhi
Phan," she said in a quiet voice.

I saw Nhi start to straighten his braces. I held my breath
and breathed a quick prayer.

Nhi grasped his crutches and walked slowly toward the
school principal. "Oh, Lord, please don't let him fall."

Students began to clap politely. No one laughed. Then
as Nhi reached the principal and shook his hand before
receiving the certificate, boys and girls all over the audito-

rium began to clap and cheer wildly. Some stood up and yelled, "Yea Nhi!"

The lump in my throat grew. Tears started streaming down my cheeks. Steve squeezed my hand, and when I turned toward him I was surprised to find his eyes were full of tears. I could count on one hand the times I had seen my husband cry in our married life. "That's my son," he whispered. I was happy to know that Steve was feeling more and more like a father. I knew his commitment to Nhi and Hy was as strong as mine, but until that moment I was not sure he shared my parental feelings.

The week after school was out, we took the boys to Rehoboth Beach in Delaware for a family vacation. Hy was somewhat cautious in the water, but Nhi rode the waves fearlessly on a rubber raft. Steve carried him out into the surf, while I caught him as he hit the beach, and held the raft until Steve arrived.

As I was waiting for Nhi to ride in again, I fell into conversation with a woman who also had two adopted children. Both children had had orthopedic problems which required corrective surgery. When she had given birth to a little girl with turned-in feet and was told of the problem by her husband, her response was, "I wouldn't know how to change a diaper on a baby who wasn't wearing leg braces!"

Her upbeat attitude toward her children's difficulties made it easy for me to tell her about our own family. She listened enthusiastically and then said, "Why, you must be having a ball with your family!" Many people had sympathized with us, or told us what a great thing we were doing for Nhi and Hy. But because of her own experiences this woman had hit on the truth. We were having a great time— and giving very little in comparison to the love and joy we were receiving.

This encouraging conversation remained in my mind as we prepared for Nhi's back operation. Our first consultations with Nhi's doctor, John Bennett, were sobering. Dr. Bennett met us at Children's Hospital, and tacked Nhi's most recent back x-rays to a lighted screen.

"My back looks like a dragon, like the shape of Vietnam," Nhi joked.

It was an astute observation. The lower part of his back-bone was on the right side of his body instead of in the center where it belonged. The top part curved toward the left, forming an "S" shape. Because his body was more affected on one side than the other, over the years the strong muscles on his right side pulled his backbone and hip out of alignment. The upper part of his back curved in the opposite direction to compensate for the bulge in the lower part. Even as we looked at the x-ray, Nhi was balancing himself on one hip and hand; his other hip was several inches above the table and appeared to be dislocated.

Dr. Bennett explained that Nhi's surgery was not optional; without it, his backbone would eventually crush his vital organs. In fact, he was surprised that tests showed there was as yet no discernible damage. He traced Nhi's vertebrae on the x-ray. "They are curved 120°," he explained. "The best we can hope for is to reduce the curve to 60°. We won't try to straighten out the compensatory curve at the top."

Dr. Bennett answered our questions about the surgery slowly and thoughtfully. "Two chest surgeons will open Nhi up with a twelve-inch incision on his back and on his chest. Then the orthopedic doctors will take over. Two will work from the front and two from the back simultaneously. We will remove the discs from between his vertebrae all the way from his shoulders to the end of his tailbone. Then we will push the backbone over as much as possible and hold it in place with screws and a Harrington rod. After several months the bones will fuse together."

I asked Dr. Bennett what could go wrong. "If we do not move the backbone enough, Nhi will still be very crooked. If we push it too far, we could damage the spinal cord. There is always the slim possibility of a disaster—a few people die from this kind of operation, and a small percent are paralyzed, some temporarily, some permanently. But for Nhi that would not be as great a tragedy since he does not have the use of his legs even now."

At this point I wanted to object, but refrained. Nhi had been walking up stairs and over curbs for six months. He had use of all his organs and bowel and bladder control.

He could move one foot enough to tap out a beat while playing the guitar or harmonica. The loss of these functions would be as great a tragedy for him as anyone else.

"Nhi can return to school four weeks after the operation," Dr. Bennett was continuing. "But it is hard to know how long it will be before he can walk again. He will wear a half-body cast for three to six months until the vertebrae fuse together. And he will need a special pass to go through airport metal detectors because the screws and wires in his back will always set them off."

Steve and I asked Nhi if he understood all that Dr. Bennett had said, and asked him if he would like to talk things over with Hy before making a final decision.

"No, Mom and Dad, Dr. Bennett explained it clearly. I want to have the operation and I'm not afraid." Although we had carefully explained to Nhi that there was less than one in a thousand chance that he would die, we later learned that he was convinced he had only a 50 percent chance of surviving the operation.

During the next few weeks, Steve and I called doctors and medical school professors around the country to get an evaluation of Children's Hospital and Dr. Bennett. All the information we received confirmed that both the hospital and the doctor were excellent choices. Nhi's dream of receiving the best medical care for his back was finally becoming a reality.

Nhi and I checked into Children's Hospital the afternoon before his operation. We spent several hours traveling from one lab to another while Nhi gave blood and urine samples, and different doctors examined him in preparation for the surgery. After the tests, Nhi and I took our overnight bags to his room. There I absentmindedly flipped through the day's mail, and discovered a just-arrived issue of *World Vision,* a magazine about relief and development efforts in the Third World.

A small article reported that rain had finally come to parched areas of East Africa. The month before our family had sent a donation to *World Vision* for its work with the hungry and thirsty refugees in that part of the world. Now as I read the good news of the rain aloud to Nhi, he clasped his hands together in the air.

"Thank you, God! You answer my prayers!" he cried. "Oh Mom, I have been praying every day for rain in Africa and now God has sent it. I am so happy."

My eyes filled with tears. Nhi was facing an operation that would put him in a half-body cast for three months and afflict him with non-stop pain for weeks. But his prayers and thoughts were with people whose problems were greater than his. I envied him his abandon toward his own needs, and I wished I had the freedom that came with his selflessness.

Nhi's bravery was infectious, and after we prayed together, we both slept peacefully. Steve had to wake us up when he arrived at the hospital in the morning. The three of us held hands and sang and prayed. Then a large orderly in light green surgical garb came to roll Nhi to the operating table. He lifted Nhi onto an oversized stretcher, and we followed Nhi to the entrance of the operating room, hugging and kissing him good-bye. Nhi was chatting cheerfully with the orderly and his doctors as he was wheeled through the double doors. Seeing his courage, I felt some of my own anxiety disappear.

Steve and I went to the surgery waiting room where a dozen other parents were sitting or talking quietly with one another. They came and went as their children's operations were completed, and Steve and I were the only ones who waited the entire day. I felt an inexplicable peace, even as the hours wore on.

Nhi's physical therapist watched most of the operation and brought us periodic reports throughout the day. "It's like an auto repair shop," she said. "The doctors are cutting and hammering on Nhi's backbone to make it straight. Dr. Bennett is incredible—he hasn't taken a break or taken his eyes off Nhi since he started!"

In the afternoon, Steve's parents arrived with Hy and Loc, and then our minister, Gordon Cosby, joined us. Other members of our church were keeping a prayer vigil throughout Nhi's operation with different people taking turns in the chapel.

Gordon asked each one of us how we were holding up. I was surprised at Hy's answer. He explained that his and Nhi's main reason for coming to America was to get Nhi's legs fixed, so that they could play soccer together. They were very sad to learn that Nhi would never walk without braces and crutches. But their second most important reason for coming to America was to get Nhi's back straightened, so they were both happy about the operation.

It was the first time that Steve and I fully understood that the boys had thought Nhi would one day be able to run and play like other boys. Nhi had hidden his disappointment well during our many visits to the brace maker and physical therapist. I wondered what other sorrows and secrets were hidden behind Nhi's and Hy's seemingly perpetually joyful countenances.

Ten hours after the surgery began, Dr. Bennett walked into the waiting room. His white surgical mask hung loosely from his neck, and he talked in a subdued voice as if he barely had enough energy to speak. "The operation went well, but Nhi did lose a lot of blood. We were able to straighten his back to 40° and he will be moved to the ICU unit in an hour or so. You can visit him there."

We felt a tremendous sense of relief. Nhi's back had been straightened 20° more than Dr. Bennett had predicted was the best he could do. I wanted to run and hold Nhi right away, and tell him the good news, but we had to wait for him to be hooked up to machines and monitors in the Intensive Care Unit.

When we finally were able to see Nhi, I was unprepared for the shock of his appearance. I had devoted all my energy to preparing for his operation, which I thought would bring an end to his suffering, but now I understood that he was now enduring a new kind of suffering. There were tubes in his nose and in his arms. There were monitors on his chest. He had two long incisions in his body, and a drainage tube in one side, as well as a catheter to expel urine. A nurse and a doctor worked silently and steadily at his side while television screens over his head pulsed with information on his heartbeat and blood pressure.

Nhi was awake and shivering. I held his hand and told him that the operation was even more successful than the doctors had hoped. Nhi didn't answer and a nurse, seeing my bewilderment, explained that the respirator tube in

Nhi's nose passed through his throat and made it impossible for him to speak.

Hy spoke to Nhi for some time. They exchanged tender glances as Hy reached out to hold Nhi's hand. I wondered what Hy was saying, and tried to imagine being in his shoes—seeing his brother in such pain, and the two of them alone in a foreign land, ten thousand miles from their home.

Later in the evening Steve drove Loc and Hy home, and I spent the night with Nhi. Every few minutes at least one of his machines was beeping for attention: the urine pouch filled, the bag collecting the drainage from his side had to be changed, the IV's needed adjusting, and his oxygen levels dropped. The nurse and doctor worked quietly and efficiently while Nhi slept fitfully. He shivered constantly and was still bleeding. I later learned he had lost nine pints of blood during surgery—twice his own volume.

I looked at the clock for the first time and noticed it was 3:00 A.M. Suddenly I was exhausted, and I realized I had been standing for five hours. I went to the waiting room and sat down in the only empty seat next to a twelve-year-old girl. She and her mother were in the second month of their vigil for her younger brother who had been running for his school bus when he was hit by an unlicensed and uninsured driver. We talked quietly. I learned that she and her mother came to visit every night, and I was moved by the compassionate and yet matter-of-fact manner with which she talked about her brother's tragedy. Her company was comforting and reassuring and I dozed for several hours.

The following days were an endless succession of eight-hour shifts in the ICU, with Steve, Hy, and me taking turns. We marked time by small signs of progress—Nhi's decreasing need for blood transfusions, his decreased dependence on the respirator, marginally smaller doses of morphine needed to ease the pain. Finally the respirator tube came out and Nhi could talk again for the first time since his operation.

These small improvements were often eclipsed by new problems. Two days after surgery, Nhi's legs began to swell. Hy noticed it first, and exclaimed that the operation had helped Nhi's legs because they were already getting bigger.

When Nhi began to complain of pain, I called a doctor walking through the ICU to look at his legs.

"Nonsense!" he exclaimed. "Those thin legs cannot possibly be swollen." He hurried away. Finally, I located the chief surgical resident who had participated in Nhi's operation, and he agreed that Nhi's legs were dangerously swollen. X-rays showed no blood clot, and the swelling eventually went down on its own.

Meanwhile, Nhi needed to be turned every hour to keep him from developing bed sores. It was no small task. His right side had a six inch tube inserted in it to drain the continual oozing from the surgery. His right hip was still healing from the bone chips the doctors had removed and inserted between his vertebrae. His left hip already had a bed sore from the nine and a half hours he had spent in surgery. His lower right rib had been severed, and his lungs were too weak for him to lie on his stomach. That left only his back, where he had an incision from his shoulders to his tail bone. We did our best to give his skin relief from the pressure of his own weight, and at the doctor's suggestions we propped up first one half of his back and then the other.

The next two weeks brought a string of frustrating and often dangerous mistakes. A nurse dragged Nhi onto scales next to his bed to weigh him, and failed to ask for assistance. When I saw Nhi afterwards, his eyes were staring straight ahead, and his jaw muscles were tight with pain. Another nurse rolled him over on his stomach to prevent bed sores on his back, and Nhi was left to lie on his severed rib, gasping for breath. An orthopedic resident failed to cut a hole in Nhi's body cast for his diaphragm to expand, and Nhi's breathing became increasingly labored. When I called that resident, he glanced at Nhi and said, "He doesn't need a hole in his cast; he just needs to learn a new way of breathing. Of course the cast feels tight in the beginning, but he'll get used to it."

I looked at Nhi's terrified face as he gasped for air and ran down the hall to call Dr. Bennett. He came immediately, took one look at Nhi, and said, "The cast needs a hole for his diaphragm!" He grabbed a saw and cut a piece out of the cast. Nhi gulped the air that rushed into his lungs, and

I was left to wonder what would have happened if Dr. Bennett had not been available.

One of the biggest problems was Nhi's medication. One of his doctors had explained to me that when Nhi's backbone was pushed over 80°, every muscle in his body had been stretched tight. The shock was comparable to falling from a three-story building. Unless Nhi got adequate amounts of morphine *on time* his muscles would be too tight for the pain medicine to work effectively.

The nurses on the orthopedic hall understood this problem and were skilled at caring for spinal fusion patients. But unfortunately, because of a case of chicken pox in the orthopedic hall, Nhi was moved to the general surgery recovery ward. None of the nurses there had experience in providing the kind of care Nhi needed, and they were continually disagreeing with the amount of morphine which the doctors prescribed. Accustomed to working with infants and toddlers recovering from routine surgery, they again and again cut Nhi's prescribed dosage of pain medicine. Every eight hours, I had to try to educate a new nurse about my son's unusual needs, and there were a series of frustrating incidents. Over and over again nurses delayed Nhi's medication until it was too late or lowered his dosage to the point that it was ineffective. Nhi hardly slept at all, and we were forced continually to call Dr. Bennett to get the nurses to follow his orders.

Events came to a head one afternoon when Nhi called us at home where we had gone for a rest. "Please, Mom and Dad, come to the hospital. Something is wrong. The nurse gave me my medicine on time, but it's not helping!"

I called the nurse on duty to find out what medication Nhi had received and when. "The doctors over-prescribed his codeine," she explained in a patient voice. I had heard the phrase a dozen times already. "So I just gave Nhi some aspirin."

Aspirin! Only two and a half weeks after an excruciating operation. I relayed the conversation to Steve, who slammed his fist on the table. "I'm sick of this!" he said angrily. "We can give Nhi better care here at home. Let's go to the hospital and get him."

I was startled at Steve's response, but as we talked it

over, I began to think bringing Nhi home might not be such a bad idea. Dr. Bennett had said that Nhi only needed to stay another week, and that was because of his need for physical therapy. His physical therapist, who had already been a tremendous help to him, would be glad to come to our house. If anything went wrong, we were only five minutes from a hospital. Nhi had not had a single night of uninterrupted rest since his operation, and while it was noisy and impersonal at the hospital, at home he would have the quiet and personal attention he needed. Most importantly, he wouldn't have to worry about his pain medicine.

I wasn't completely convinced. Kidnapping one's son from the hospital seemed to be an overly desperate act. But Steve was persuasive, and the thought of Nhi's continual pain made a strong case for bold action. Finally, I agreed. Together with Hy we planned our rescue operation, and within a short time we were on our way to the hospital.

15
STEVE

A Daring Escape

Debi, Hy, and I piled into our car and sped down the George Washington Parkway toward the hospital. I pressed the accelerator to the floor and hoped that the police wouldn't pick us up for speeding.

I was seething with rage. Every few hours for the past seventeen days we had to battle the nursing staff to get Nhi his pain medicine. His only escape from non-stop agony was sleep, which he desperately needed. Yet almost every hour he was awakened one or more times to have his temperature taken, to be given a laxative, to take another pill. Once when he had just fallen asleep after hours of wakefulness, a nurse came in with his lunch. When Debi protested and offered to feed him later, the nurse responded, "He can't start thinking he can eat and sleep whenever he wants to." Once again, Nhi was awakened to a world of pain and sleeplessness.

It had been an uphill battle all the way for Nhi, and now this. A young woman who worked primarily with newborn babies decided on her own that all Nhi needed after a massive back operation was aspirin! I started to calm down only when I considered the benefits to Nhi of having him at home, where he could get the personal care and quiet that he needed. I looked over at Debi. From the worried tone in her voice I could tell that she was still scared by the idea of kidnapping Nhi from the hospital. But I knew that she was also cheered by the prospect of finally having him home.

Instead of parking in the underground lot beneath the hospital, I pulled around to the back and parked illegally

at the service entrance. I left the car lights flashing as if
we were making a delivery. We ran to Nhi's room and in
an excited whisper I announced, "You're going home today,
Nhi! In fact, we're going home right now!"

Debi stayed in the room with Nhi while Hy and I piled
up the wheelchair with all the flowers, plants, cards, and
gifts which people sent. We made two trips to the car. Then,
just as I had done during my last few visits, I gently lifted
Nhi from his bed to his wheelchair. As we prepared the
final plan for "lift-off" I casually walked down to the nurses'
refrigerator and helped myself to four grape popsicles. Then
I handed the booty to Nhi who hid them under the clothes
in his lap. "To make sure no nurses come by your room,
Nhi, maybe we should buzz the station and ask for your
pain medicine." I winked at Debi. We all laughed nervously.

Before we made our escape Debi checked to make sure
there were no nurses on the hall. It was empty. She then
walked to the end of the wing and peeked around the corner. The coast was clear. She motioned for Nhi, Hy, and
me to follow. We walked down the hall away from the
nurses' station and then waited for the slow employees'
elevator. Our hearts pounded loudly. I was sure that we
would be discovered before the elevator arrived.

Finally the doors opened, and we dashed inside. I suddenly felt more optimistic. As soon as we reached the first
floor, we wheeled Nhi past the emergency room and out
to the car, which fortunately was still where I parked it.
We lifted Nhi carefully onto pillows in the front seat.

As I started the engine and pulled away from the curb,
we all cheered and laughed, and sucked on our grape popsicles. "We should be on 'Mission Impossible,'" I said, forget-
ting that this well-known television show was part of
American culture that the boys had never experienced. Nhi
was ecstatic. He grinned from ear to ear and played his
favorite song on his harmonica. It was the well-loved Vietnamese ballad, "Return to Your Country." It had a new
meaning now for the Standiford-Phan family—"Return to
Arlington County."

"What does our home look like now?" Nhi asked.

"What do you mean? It's the same as when you left," I

replied. "You've only been gone two and a half weeks!"

"I know, but it seems like I've been at the hospital so long that everything will be changed by now."

Strangely, during our entire rescue mission, no one asked us where we were going. We signed no papers. We were later informed that Nhi's hospital records stated he left the hospital "AMA"—Against Medical Advice. Not against medical advice, I thought to myself. But because medical advice for Nhi's pain medication was seldom followed.

We made a bed for Nhi on our living room sofa bed. I called Dr. Bennett at home and explained that we had brought our son home so that he could get his pain medication. I assured him that Nhi would get his physical therapy. Dr. Bennett apologized for the problems we had encountered. Then I called our family physician, Janelle Goetcheus, who prescribed Nhi's codeine. We gave it to him according to her orders, and Nhi slept well Saturday night for the first time since before his operation.

Nhi's demand for pain medication decreased rapidly over the next few days. He no longer had to guess how long it would take for him to receive his next dose, and with the knowledge that he could have a pill whenever he needed it, he began to voluntarily stretch the time between doses. His muscles stayed relaxed, and the medicine was substantially more effective.

Nhi met with his physical therapist, Jan Tropp, nearly every day, and he and Debi carefully followed the regimen they had learned in the hospital. Because the spinal fusion had changed the length of one of Nhi's legs, he had to have his braces adjusted, and the height of the lift on his shoes changed several times. Still, within two weeks, with the encouragement and enthusiasm of Jan, Nhi was able to walk from the first to the second floor of our home. Every movement was painful, but his effort and determination paid off. We all applauded wildly as he reached the top of the stairs.

Our initial excitement was followed by unexpected frustrations. Nhi was sitting up in bed one day when he suddenly flopped over. He was overcome by a wave of dizziness and lost all control over his body. It was the first of many such attacks, and although doctors performed countless tests to determine their cause, nothing was ever uncovered. Four months later, in December, Nhi's dizziness subsided as mysteriously as it had appeared.

We were all disappointed by the length of time Nhi was forced to remain in his wheelchair. He had tasted freedom during five months of walking with crutches. Why was he so slow to walk again? It was only later that we learned why Dr. Bennett had been so vague about what kind of progress we would expect from Nhi. He had never before operated on such a curved back. Children in America had their backs corrected long before they curved as dangerously as Nhi's. Any children Dr. Bennett had seen whose curves were almost as bad as Nhi's were permanently confined to wheelchairs.

Even before his operation, the effort of walking with braces and crutches had put a great deal of strain on Nhi's back. Now the muscles attached to his backbone had been stretched and pulled, and his back was permanently fused in a relatively straight line. He could no longer balance by arching his back; instead, he was forced to discover a new center of balance. With his braces locked at the knees, falls were inevitable. Nhi had several serious spills, and he did not walk again on a regular basis until April, 1982, eight months after his operation.

The three months Nhi spent in a half body cast must have been a nightmare, but through it all, he never complained. Not once. The summer heat added to his discomfort, and often his chest and back itched as if a colony of red ants had taken up residence in his cast. Sometimes he used a tie and hanger combination to try to relieve the itching, but always he endured his pain with the stoicism which seemed so ingrained in Vietnamese men. Debi repeatedly said it would be less heart-breaking to take care of Nhi if only he *would* complain. My cousin overheard her and sent Nhi a "Peanuts" get well card: "Crab a little—it will make it easier on everyone!"

During the fall semester following his operation, Nhi struggled to keep up at school. His pain was greater when he was sitting than when he was lying down, so he regularly spent his lunch time in the school clinic. Debi and I worried that Nhi's difficulties might make him fall behind his class, and we began to wonder if he would be able to graduate at the end of the semester into a full day of regular classes held in English.

It was during this time that Debi and I began to have disagreements about how to best help Nhi overcome his latest setback. We spent many hours lying awake at night trying to figure out how to support and encourage both boys to do their best. Debi accused me of pushing Nhi and Hy too hard to do well in school—in the same way I had been pushed when I was growing up. She thought Nhi needed more time to recover completely from his back operation before he worried about school work.

For my part, I thought Debi was too lenient. I insisted that I was only looking out for Nhi's best interests, and he had to learn to take responsibility for his own life. The semiannual test for foreign students which allowed them to pass out of their special classes into regular classes was coming up soon. If Nhi failed, he would have to spend another semester in the English-as-a-second-language program.

It was a disagreement we never fully worked out. Finally, we just had to accept our differences, and hope that somehow together our two different approaches provided a healthy atmosphere for Hy and Nhi in the special circumstances which surrounded their lives. Sometimes we laughed together as we realized how easily we had fallen into traditional roles—I as challenger, Debi as comforter.

I did have to admit that much of my own ego had become tied up in how well Nhi and Hy were doing. It was nice to have people marvel at the rapid progress they had made in little over a year. At the same time it was clear that, although Debi and I drilled Nhi and Hy in English at home, their remarkable progress was due primarily to their own hard work and to the excellent teachers who taught English as a foreign language at Washington-Lee High School. These outstanding teachers were epitomized by Terry Bratt, the head of the department. She was energetic and demanding—and she understood how difficult it was for foreign students to learn English. Through repetition, oral drills, and a heavy emphasis on memorization, she helped hundreds of students in the classroom. Then on her own time, she spent many hours tutoring students who needed extra help. She and her husband sponsored social activities in their home for foreign students, who often had difficulty socializing with American teenagers. Terry also sponsored the Vietnamese Club, which had more than seventy members—including Nhi and Hy!

Despite his physical difficulties, by January Nhi seemed ready for his English exam. He was doing more and more for himself physically, and he seemed cheerful and confident. At the same time, Hy was becoming less protective and more willing to let Nhi make his own way. Our personal lives were settling down some, and Loc and his sister (who had been living with us since her arrival from the refugee camps in October) had struck out on their own during the Christmas holiday. They found a small apartment near Loc's fiancée, and although we were sorry to see them go, we were grateful for the extra room.

At the end of January, Nhi was one of only a handful of students who passed the exam. We celebrated at our local Chinese restaurant, and toasted Nhi's hard work. In just a few weeks he would join other American students in a full day of regular classes.

A few days later we celebrated again. This time it was for Tet, the Vietnamese New Year. As usual we went to the local Vietnamese Tet bazaar and bought sticky rice wrapped in banana leaves, a duck roasted with special Vietnamese spices, and many tiny spring rolls (the Vietnamese version of egg rolls).

Debi and I had decided that as part of our Tet celebration we would take Nhi and Hy to the Buddhist temple for the Tet worship service. It was something we had talked and prayed about at length. We wanted Nhi and Hy to share in the good news of Jesus Christ, to share our own faith. Yet we did not believe that cutting them off from their own spiritual roots was the answer.

During Nhi's and Hy's first year in America, we had often offered to take them to the Buddhist temple so that they could participate in services there. Our offers were always met with protests. Nhi and Hy said they only went to the Buddhist temple on special occasions in Vietnam, and it was not necessary to go at other times. Father Joe had told us that Nhi and Hy would probably do anything to please us—including not going to the temple if they thought that was what we really wanted.

To show Nhi and Hy that we loved and accepted them even if they remained Buddhists, we resolved to take them to the Tet service—over their objections, if necessary. To our surprise, they seemed excited and happy about the four of us going as a family.

The service was held at midnight in a house a few miles from our home. We arrived early, but the house was already filled with people. At six feet, I towered over most of the Vietnamese in the room. The older women gathered in one corner to talk quietly, while children giggled and darted in and out of the congregation. In the living room was a life-sized Buddha sitting on an altar loaded with incense and fruit.

A young monk in his mid-thirties wearing a saffron robe and a shaved head approached us and in broken English offered us coffee and doughnuts while we waited for the service to begin. He seemed genuinely pleased that we had brought Nhi and Hy to the service. A short while later he personally escorted us upstairs to the temple sanctuary. The sanctuary—two small bedrooms with an interior wall removed—held about eighty people. By the time the service began the house was overflowing with people—on the stairs, in the halls, even in the kitchen. Debi and I knelt shoulder to shoulder near the back of the room, while the monk took Nhi up to the front and put him on a chair near the altar. I was touched at the special attention which Nhi received.

During the service we read Vietnamese transliterations of Hindi prayers. Hy explained that no one understood the words that they were praying. The foreign language, incense, and large crowd, along with the lateness of the hour, made the service seem very much like the midnight Latin mass which I attended as a boy each year on Christmas

Eve. The big difference was the larger-than-life gold Buddha sitting on the altar surrounded by hundreds of oranges and apples.

Just before the service ended, the monks said a special prayer for Nhi. After one and a half hours of kneeling I was glad to finally stand up, and I wondered how the older people managed. As we departed, the monks offered everyone fruit and "li xi"—little red envelopes with money inside.

On the ride home, Hy was overjoyed and talked enthusiastically about the service. "Oh, Dad, Mom, it is wonderful to see you do our custom at Tet."

"I'm glad we were able to learn a little Buddhist tradition, Hy, since that is part of who you are," I replied.

"Me too," Nhi said, with apparent sincerity. "I'm glad we went to the temple tonight."

It wasn't long before we learned how little truth was in his statement.

16
NHI

Alone

The New Year's service at the Buddhist temple last week was a nightmare for me. I was so humiliated. The monks told me to sit on a chair at the front of the room, and thousands of eyes were watching me. I wanted to kneel on the floor with Hy and Mom and Dad, like everyone else, but instead I was trapped by my paralyzed legs. When the monks prayed for me, they were condescending and made it clear how hopeless my situation was. I tried to pray to Buddha to blot out their words, but I could not concentrate.

It was just one more shadow in the darkness that is growing around me. When I first came to America, many good things happened to me, but now it seems my life has come to a dead end. I try to act happy all the time so no one will know how helpless I feel, but I am really afraid of many things.

I don't know if I will ever be able to walk again like I did before my back operation. Although I thought I might die on the operating table, I was not upset. But the long recovery was another matter. I had so much pain and dizziness it was hard to concentrate on my lessons at school. When the pain went away, I still couldn't walk. Sometimes I tried but my leg muscles were so tight that I couldn't stand up straight. It was much faster to learn to walk the first time, but now I tried and tried, and couldn't get it. My friends at school think I am lazy because I just sit in my wheelchair all the time.

I passed the exam given to students in the half-day English-as-a-second-language program, and next week I will have to take all regular classes with American students. The courses I take now are really hard. I don't think my English is good enough to be with Americans all day. None of these Americans had polio, and their brains have not been damaged like mine.

On top of these things, now I have to do everything for myself. Loc, who helped me all the time, moved into his own apartment during Christmas vacation. I miss his sister, too, who sewed my clothes and cooked wonderful Vietnamese food. Now Hy cooks dinner during the week, but Mom and Dad say next month I must start taking a turn too. They are very unfair to make me do all these things I never did before.

The worst part is that Hy is following Mom's and Dad's new way. Hy has the duty to help me, and now he has stopped. I don't even know who this guy Hy is anymore. He is so perfect. Mom and Dad love him more than me, because he is not a burden to them.

When I first came to America, Mom and Dad loved me very much. Mom took care of me just like Ma did in Vietnam. Now no one takes care of me, and no one loves me. They say they will not take care of me the rest of my life, and in a few years I will be on my own. They say I have to learn to do things for myself. They always push me, and I am always scared. They even make me clean the bathrooms—just like I am a servant and not a son.

In Vietnam, my family would always have protected me. Ma and Ba were putting money in the bank for my future. But now we are apart, and it looks like we will never be together again. Their letters from Vietnam are full of sad news, and they are hungry and poor. But Hy and I cannot sponsor them to come to America because we said we were orphans. This lie has turned out bad in every way, but if the truth is told I will become a beggar on the street. Not like Hy. He can take care of himself.

Sometimes when I think about my handicap, I think, *Why me? Why does every other child get to run and play, but I have these shriveled legs? God, why did you do this to me? I don't deserve this heavy burden on my shoulders.*

Then I remember what I learned in Vietnam. In a previous life I refused to give a crippled beggar some money.

In my imagination, I often see myself as a very fat, rich, powerful Chinese man dressed in flowing, floor-length gowns and living in a large house with shiny marble floors. One day I walk outside of my big front door, somehow knowing that there is a beggar there. The beggar is the same age as I. He is dressed only in short pants, and has thin hideous legs with skin stretched across his leg bones. The rich man who is me stomps powerfully on the beggar and kicks him, and the beggar rolls into the gutter on the edge of the street. Now in this life I am that crippled beggar.

Sometimes I wonder why I have to pay for the sins of someone I don't even remember. And I wonder if handicapped people in America have the same history as I do. When I see a person here in a wheelchair, I cannot look him in the eye. I think, *Who is this guy in the wheelchair?* It makes me sad to know that their life is so difficult. I would rather it be just me, and not them too.

I used to have the idea that after my legs were fixed here in America then I could do everything. So I waited for that day to come. But it never came.

Lately, I haven't really wanted to get out of bed in the morning. That makes Hy very upset; because he pushes my wheelchair to school, then he is late too. This morning he just went without me. And Dad yelled at me. He said he was angry because I was late for school, but I think he is angry because he is starting to realize what a burden I am. I fall down too many times, and I can't say the difficult words like "the." Mom and Dad have to do so many things for me, I think they are tired of having me in the family.

Tonight, Mom is not here, and Dad and Hy went to watch a basketball game without me. I have never been punished before by Mom or Dad, but Dad said I have to stay home and go to bed early so I can get up in the morning.

Now that I am all alone, so many sad thoughts come into my head. I compare myself to Hy, and I see that my brother never gets into trouble. He can walk and does well in school. But he will not take me to school anymore when I am late. Everyone has left me here, and Ma and Ba are far away. I am alone with my braces and crutches, and I am a burden even to myself.

I cry for a long time, and all I can think is that no one

loves me, not Mom, not Dad, not even Hy. When you feel like that your heart hurts a lot and your stomach hurts, and your throat feels choked and the tears keep falling out. I cannot do anything. I feel worthless and sad.

I remember other times in my life when I felt this way and thought about killing myself. Then I lacked courage, but now I think of how it will be when I am reincarnated with strong legs. I will run like other boys, and I will never laugh at a handicapped person. People will admire me because I am strong and full of compassion.

With these thoughts, I crawl downstairs. I look through the bottles in the bathroom cabinet until I see the words "Poison—Do Not Drink." I take the can out and open it. Then I cry and cry, and start to be scared. But I go to the telephone and write a note to Mom and Dad and Hy.

I do not want to die slowly, so I pour a lot of poison into the palm of my hand. I stop for a moment and think: *Maybe I should not eat this.* But something inside me tells me to go ahead. I put my hand quickly to my lips, and force the powder inside. It burns my tongue and mouth, and then my throat and chest.

Suddenly the telephone rings and I want so bad to answer it. I know it is Mom calling home. I want to tell her that I took poison, so that she can come and save me. But I cannot crawl to the phone. For a minute I am crazy. I claw hysterically at the walls and beat on my chest. The pain in my chest is so hot I think my heart will stop at any second. I imagine the poison going into my veins and traveling to my heart. Now I am going to die. My heart is stopping. It is almost over.

I am full of regret. If I die I cannot pay back Mom and Dad for all they have done for me. My family in Vietnam will be so sad. What will Hy do without me?

Suddenly I desperately want to live, and I put my fingers down my throat. I vomit a little, and then I try again. This time nothing happens. My body is shaking violently, and I am becoming weaker and weaker. I collapse on the floor, and see the note I wrote. I will lie down now and die.

17
DEBI

Seventeen Years of Sadness

The day began in such an ordinary way. The boys went to school as usual, although Nhi was late again. When Steve and I left for work, I told him I would be working late that evening. I was only working part time now that we had two teenage sons, but the case I was working on needed some extra attention.

In the evening, Steve and Hy left to watch a basketball game at Steve's parents. Nhi was asked to stay at home so that he would not be late the next morning. Although in the year and a half that the boys had been with us we had never had to punish them for anything, Nhi's chronic lateness was beginning to wear on us all. Steve hoped that a small restriction would help Nhi understand his need to be on time.

I tried to call Nhi several times throughout the evening, but there was no answer. I thought perhaps he had gone to bed early, and I hoped he was not feeling too sad about being left home alone. Even though I knew Nhi could take care of himself I began to worry that he had fallen and hurt himself. I thought of calling our neighbor, Carol, who had a key to our house, but as I looked up her number I realized how overly concerned I was. Nhi had no doubt gone to bed; if Carol opened the door she would only frighten him, and interrupt the extra sleep he needed.

After dropping Hy off at home, Steve picked me up at the office. I still felt worried about Nhi, but I did not want to admit my vague uneasiness. I was the "worrier" in our family, and I had been wrong so many times before, I knew that I could not act on every passing fear that I might feel.

As soon as we pulled onto our street, I saw a police car parked by our townhouse. My heart beat faster even as I assured Steve they were probably visiting one of our neighbors. Steve bounded up the steps and opened the door to see Hy and a uniformed policeman and policewoman standing in our hallway. The floor was covered with muddy tracks and Hy was distraught.

"Nhi swallowed poison. He was lying on the floor when I came in the house, and I called the rescue squad and our grandparents. The ambulance has already taken Nhi to the hospital!" Hy blurted out in a staccato voice.

"Your son left a suicide note," the policewoman said. She held a wrinkled scrap of paper in her hand. *To everyone who loves me,* it read. *I am sorry I cause much trouble for everyone. It's time for me to go home to God. Love, Nhi.*

I started to shake. My face felt hot and my throat constricted, but no tears came. We called our family doctor and then drove the few blocks to the hospital. Steve carried with him a large orange plastic cup which had "The University of Virginia" stamped on the outside. There was a white crusty film inside, and I wondered if Nhi had used the cup to mix up the drain cleaner.

When we arrived in the emergency room Steve's parents were already there. Steve and I rushed to Nhi's hospital room and Nhi stared at us groggily from his bed. He seemed so small and frail.

"Nhi, we love you and want you to live," I blurted out.

"I want to die, I want to die. Please go away."

Nhi's response stunned me. Steve took his other hand and told Nhi that we loved him and didn't want him to leave us.

"Please tell the doctors to go away," Nhi said emphatically. "I don't want them to help me. I want to die."

Underneath Nhi's bed I could see the can of drain cleaner and the clothes which rescue squad workers had cut from his body. A doctor and nurse walked over to us and asked if we knew why Nhi had ingested a lethal poison. "I don't know." The voice that came out of my mouth sounded as if it came from somewhere else other than my body.

Everything had seemed just fine, I explained. Nhi had passed his exam to enter regular English classes at school. The excruciating pain from his back operation had finally subsided. He was out of his cast, and he was making progress toward walking again. The only thing it could be was that he wasn't allowed to watch the basketball game because he was late for school.

"Are you sure that was it?" the doctor asked in a puzzled voice. I told him it made no sense to me either, but I couldn't think of any other explanation.

I was called to the telephone in the waiting room. It was the first of several calls from members of our church. Two people who had worked in the refugee camp, David Williams and Helen Cary, came by to visit and joined Steve's parents. The presence of family members and friends was both a comfort and a shame. Soon everyone would know that my son had attempted suicide. Everyone would know I was a failure as a mother. I thought of an acquaintance I knew whose son had killed himself. At the time I had wondered whether his son would still be alive if he had been a better father and spent less time at work. Now on the very evening I worked late. . . . Perhaps if I had stayed at home none of this would have happened.

I thought Nhi would be glad to see Helen and David. He was not. He was remote and withdrawn and I found myself feeling detached from him as well. But I kept going back to his bed to tell him we loved him and wanted him to live. It was as if I were a robot going through motions— talking to doctors, comforting Nhi, answering the telephone, and trying to make appropriate responses to questions. A sense of horrified calm enveloped me.

Dr. Gabriel Herman, a gastroenterologist, decided to look down Nhi's stomach with an endoscope to determine whether the drain cleaner had eaten through the stomach lining. He carefully explained the procedure to us and was gentle and caring with Nhi. He even joked with him as he guided the tube down his throat. I was grateful that he did not appear angry for being called back to the hospital so late at night.

There was no tear in Nhi's stomach lining. He had passed

out before he had eaten much of the powder. I remembered all the time I had told Nhi and Hy how strong our household cleaners were, and how only a little bit could make them very sick. Had my warnings helped or hurt? Did Nhi take only a little because he thought that much would kill him? Or would he have taken it at all if it hadn't been for my stern warnings?

I returned to the waiting room feeling more dazed and defeated than before. I felt like I had the plague. I assumed everyone around me was wondering what kind of mother I was that my adopted son should try and kill himself. It occurred to me that I was more worried about what people were thinking than my son's recovery, and this thought seemed only further proof of my inadequacies as a mother.

A middle-aged nurse with a kind face came toward me. "Honey, you've been standing up too long. Have a seat and I'll bring you some coffee." She put her arm around me and guided me to a chair. For the first time all evening I felt close to tears.

At three A.M. the doctor and nurse suggested we all go home. They promised to call if there were any changes in Nhi's condition. Unlike our previous hospital experience during Nhi's back operation, we felt complete confidence in the medical staff, and knew it was unnecessary to keep a round-the-clock vigil.

When we arrived home, we pulled Hy's mattress into our bedroom so that he would not have to be alone. Steve and Hy were soon asleep, but I lay awake until morning trying to understand why Nhi wanted to die.

When Steve and I returned to the hospital, Nhi was silent. He seemed worse than the night before, and I did not know how to respond. I walked out into the waiting room and saw Mary Cosby, our minister's wife. "Dear one, we've been praying for you," she said in her comforting and cultured Southern accent. Over coffee she explained to me that I had a right to be angry at Nhi. I didn't know what she was saying. I was angry with myself; why would I be angry with my son? Despite my confusion, I was happy to see that Mary still loved and respected me—even though she knew I was the mother of a teenage boy who had tried to kill himself.

I sat with Nhi most of the day. I kept telling him that we loved him and needed him and would miss him too much if he died. There was no response, and I couldn't think of anything else to say.

In the afternoon, I met Hy when he came home from school, and tried to talk with him about what had happened the night before. "Mom," he said. "I was home alone when I found Nhi. I don't want to talk about it. I want to forget it!" But later in the afternoon, Hy was more communicative. "I was so afraid Nhi would be dead when we got to the hospital. All I could see in my mind was his body lying on the floor, half in the bathroom, half in the hallway. When you told me I had done all the right things when I found him, that it was good to call '911' and the grandparents, I felt better. It helped me to know that you and Dad thought everything was going to be okay."

When I arrived at Nhi's room the next morning, a Vietnamese social worker was just leaving. She smiled encouragingly, and I said a silent prayer that Nhi would talk to me. It made me deeply afraid not to know what he was thinking or feeling.

Nhi stared at the wall stoically as I said good morning and gave him a kiss. Then he abruptly started to speak.

"Do you think I am a child or an adult?"

I was startled and hoped I could respond correctly. "In some ways you seem older than seventeen and in other ways younger," I said matter-of-factly. "Your English is not as good as most American teenagers, but your actions make you seem older. You have a great deal of love and understanding, and you are more patient and forgiving than the average American boy your age."

"I hate it when people call me a child," Nhi said vehemently. "Do you think I am lazy?"

I had never heard him speak so directly. "No," I responded, "I don't think you are lazy. You have a lot of courage, and it's not an easy task to walk with crutches."

"Oh, Mom, my friends at school tease me about being lazy because I have been in the wheelchair so long since my operation." Nhi was choking back tears and only shook his head when I asked him who had teased him.

We were both quiet for a moment. Finally I asked a question which had been haunting me since the night of Nhi's suicide attempt. "Nhi, did you swallow that drain cleaner because of what happened the night before last, or did seventeen years of sadness just become too much?"

Nhi was silent for a long time. I held my breath. Then suddenly he rolled over and threw his splinted, I.V.-laden arm over my shoulder. He put his head against my chest and sobbed. He wept for several minutes while I was quiet. Then I tried to console him with words I do not remember.

A nurse walked in and adjusted Nhi's intravenous tube. She hardly seemed to notice us. Now I was crying too, and Nhi handed me a Kleenex. It was good to release the tears that had seemed so strangely absent in the last two days.

Nhi's words tumbled out as if his sobbing had unplugged seventeen years of bottled up sadness. "In America I was happy because I could walk and do things for myself. But it has been hard to be in a wheelchair again. I make so many mistakes, and I feel like I am a burden to everyone." Nhi explained the terrible fear that he felt in the Gulf of Thailand when the pirates forced everyone off the boat except for him. When the pirates' boat began to pull away, Nhi understood with horrifying insight how vulnerable and dependent he was. From that point on his biggest fear had been who would take care of him. When he saw Hy and his new parents pushing him to take care of himself, his terrifying fear of being abandoned only intensified.

At any other time, I would have assured Nhi that he would indeed one day be able to take care of himself. Now I told him that Steve and I and Hy would always be there if he needed us. And if something should happen to us, Steve's parents had promised to take care of both him and Hy.

As Nhi continued to talk, I realized that he was convinced that all of us would heave a sigh of relief when he was gone. His suicide had not been an attention-getting stunt. He fully intended to kill himself, and when he discovered he had failed, he was embarrassed. His effort to ease our burden had clearly only burdened us more.

In the next few days, we began to understand even better the currents that had come so close to sweeping Nhi away. The social worker explained to us how deeply Nhi missed the love of his aunt and uncle. They had loved him as a child, and done everything for him because he would not be able to take care of himself in Vietnamese society. The adult love that came from Steve and me was confusing to Nhi because he had never before been pushed to be self-sufficient. She said that Nhi was beginning to understand this new way, and we should continue to encourage him to take care of himself.

We learned too that in Vietnamese society, handicapped people were often despised and rejected by their families. Frequently they were thrown out to be beggars on the street. If a family loved a handicapped child, the way they demonstrated their love was to do everything possible for their injured family member. To ask a handicapped person to do chores was to threaten him or her with a withdrawal of love and a life of beggary. For the first time we learned how terrible Nhi felt about cleaning the bathroom.

This news about Vietnamese attitudes toward the handicapped was especially surprising. I had assumed that while Nhi might have trouble with his American peers, the Vietnamese had always lovingly accepted him as an equal. Now I recalled the stares we normally received in Vietnamese restaurants. On those occasions my son was being publicly humiliated and ostracized, but we had not understood the depth of his suffering. Even the Tet service at the Buddhist temple which we assumed to be a special treat for Nhi had been an agony for him.

We also learned from the social worker that Nhi was deeply worried about how he would repay Steve and me for everything we had done for him. In Vietnam, giving was always a two-way street, and even the gift of one grain of rice was not allowed to go unreciprocated. It was a question of honor, and Nhi felt that he was permanently dishonored by our gifts to him.

It was a rude lesson in cross-cultural relationships. The very things Steve and I had done to express our love for Nhi and Hy had become barriers between us. From the beginning we were determined not to "coddle" Nhi, and we required the same contribution from him to the household as came from Hy. We assumed that this would communicate to Nhi the depths of our respect and love for him, and that he would understand that we saw him, like Hy, as a person rather than a boy with a handicap. But the very things we did to say "I love you" to Nhi came back to him as "We don't love you, and your days here are numbered."

I wished that we had learned about these cultural differences much earlier, and we began to encourage Nhi and Hy to express themselves more. We explained to them that because of the difference in our background and culture, we would never understand each other adequately unless we began to talk freely about our thoughts and feelings. Nhi still seemed somewhat depressed, but he began to talk more freely.

While Nhi was still in the hospital, I told him about a lesson I had learned about Christian giving from an African minister. Giving, the pastor explained, is not a two-way street. Instead it is an endless stream. We may receive many gifts from people whom we are never able to repay. Our task is not to repay but to pass on what we have received. I explained to Nhi that Steve and I did not expect him and Hy to pay us back. But we hoped that someday after they finished their schooling, they would consider helping other people. Perhaps they would even lend a hand to other Vietnamese who were new in America.

After a week and a half under observation in the hospital, Nhi came home. We returned to the hospital for several more checkups, but his stomach healed without the need for surgery. I still worried that there were unhealed emotional scars for Nhi, and I was just beginning to digest the extent of Vietnamese prejudice against the handicapped. What extraordinary difficulties Nhi had faced in his first sixteen years! It was absurd to think that in sixteen months, Steve and I could give him enough love to erase all the pain of his past. But I found myself still trying. I knew that Nhi was already a young man and a well-formed person, and that our communication, now more than ever, must be adult to adult. Yet I felt in my heart that God intended to bring us together as a family—across thousands of miles and through barriers of culture and language—and that somehow through our experiences together, all of us would grow more fully into the people we were created to be.

18
NHI

First Love

The last thing I remember after drinking the drain cleaner is a voice speaking from far away. Then someone was shaking me and cutting off my sweatshirt.

When I woke up in the hospital, a doctor was putting a tube in my body. I was so embarrassed. I had wanted to stop making trouble for Mom and Dad, but now there was more trouble than ever. I told the doctors to go away, because I knew if they fixed me, then Mom and Dad would still have to take care of me.

Then I had some long talks with Mom and Dad and a social worker. She explained to me that my American mother and father wanted to encourage me to be independent, but they still loved me. They wanted what was best for me. I started thinking about her ideas. Before, sometimes I trusted Mom and Dad and sometimes I didn't. But I started to feel that maybe what they were saying was true.

When I came home from the hospital, I decided to try an experiment. I was tired of all the pushing from Mom and Dad, so I just went ahead and did things for myself before they reminded me. Gradually, this new way began to make sense.

It was a happy time. I started to get up first in the mornings and cook Chinese noodles for breakfast. Then I woke up Hy and we ate together. I felt very close to Hy, but I could see now that our relationship was not the same as it was in Vietnam. There we did everything together—played soccer in the house, took showers, listened to music, went downtown to eat "che," our favorite dessert made with beans and ice. In fact, I never went anywhere without

Hy or someone in my family because I could not walk or ride a bicycle, and I had no wheelchair or crutches. And I always obeyed everyone in my family because I depended on them for everything.

Here in America there are many things that pull brothers apart. There are after-school activities, movies, television, and sports. But what pulls Hy and me apart most is my independence. I have started to disobey him because I don't have to worry that he will stop taking care of me if he is angry. I go places with my own friends, and sometimes they are not Hy's friends. I still love Hy very much, but I see that each person must have a life to live for himself.

I am not the same person I was in Vietnam. There I always thought about how I looked. I wore long pants to cover my legs. And I was so happy the first time I got a pair of real shoes because then no one could see my feet. I was extremely self-conscious in Vietnam, but it was pointless. No one even recognized me. No one came to see me.

Now in my school people come up to me and ask me many questions. Even Vietnamese students talk to me. One of my best friends is Bich Ngoc, a Vietnamese girl who is blind. I carry her tray in the cafeteria, and everyone stares at us. I can see them out of the corner of my eye. I hold Bich Ngoc's tray on my lap and wheel to the table. She walks next to me and puts her hand on my wheelchair handle. Then I turn my head and look at all the people staring at us. I just smile at them. Then everybody smiles back at me.

Not long ago I also had a special girlfriend. During my first year in America, a beautiful Vietnamese girl tried to be my friend, but I did not understand why she liked me. I was not very friendly with her and she went away. But this time was different.

This is how it happened. One day in the cafeteria, I felt someone watching me. When I turned around, an American girl in a yellow shirt was looking at me. I couldn't believe it. I was shocked. She was so beautiful. I looked back down at my lunch so she would not catch my eyes. When I lifted my head again, she smiled and nodded. Then she walked over to talk with Bich Ngoc.

I wheeled over to Bich Ngoc. She and the American girl

were talking about braille. Just as Bich Ngoc started to intro-
duce me, the bell rang. All I learned about the girl in the
yellow shirt was that her name was Diana. I felt great. I
was really in love.

The next day, it happened again. Diana smiled at me,
and we started to talk together. She told me about her
family and I told her about mine. I learned that Diana had
a lot of sadness in her life too. But now she was living with
an aunt who loved her very much.

For Diana's birthday I made a drawing on a hollowed-
out egg. "Oh my gosh, Nhi," she said, "that's so wonderful,
can I give you a kiss?" It seemed like I was shaking. I never
expected her to do it. I didn't say anything, but she kissed
me anyway. My face got all red, and so did hers.

The next day on the way from history class to lunch,
Diana looked at me very gently. "Nhi," she began, "I have
something to tell you. But I am really shy." My stomach
started growling. Then she gave me a note. "Nhi, you are
a very nice person," it read, "and a very special person
to me. You took part of my heart."

A few days later, I was studying in the school library
when she came up behind me and kissed me again. We
started to meet in the library before school. We talked on
the phone every day. Mom and Dad complained that they
could never get through when they tried to call home. But
it seemed that I had only been talking to Diana for a few
minutes. She was the first girl who listened to me. She could
understand me and my ideas. She even learned a few Vietnamese words.

Over the summer Diana moved away. Our love had to
turn to friendship. She cried and wrote me a beautiful letter.
It was still a shock to me. I never thought I could have a
girlfriend.

During this time, I also started to think more about God.
In Vietnam, my mother had read me stories about Jesus,
even though our family was Buddhist. I had especially liked
the story of the prodigal son. But as I grew older, I came
to hate Bible stories because they were not my religion.
One day, I collected all Ma's Christian books together and
threw them out into the street.

Now I started to listen to our minister, Gordon Cosby,

and I even prayed to Jesus. It was not like praying to Buddha. Buddha is like a king; you have to be good and holy, and wear clean clothes and take a bath to speak to him. He is not a friend, and there is no forgiveness, only punishment. But Jesus seemed more like a real person to me. I could talk to him, and he would forgive me for the bad things I did. I even started to pray by myself, and with Mom and Dad at dinner and bedtime.

Now when people ask me what religion I am, I always answer, "Christian and Buddhist." Most people say they can't understand that. But I believe in both. I still wear the special sacred cloth the woman blessed for us just before we left Vietnam. But I also wear a silver cross around my neck.

I have started to tell Mom and Dad about my life in Vietnam and how difficult it is there for handicapped children. They are shocked. They thought Vietnamese people were kind and loving toward handicapped people, much kinder than Americans.

One evening after Mom and I washed the dishes together I was walking upstairs with my crutches. Mom asked me if the reason my friends were from many different countries but not Vietnam was because of the way people treated me in my own country. "Yes, Mom, you understand me," I answered. I was so glad she finally understood me. She said she wished I had told her those things before. But it was too difficult for me to talk about them. Now it seems so easy to say exactly how I feel.

19
STEVE

"You Can Do Anything"

It is hard to believe that Nhi is the same shy, self-conscious kid who arrived on his brother's back at National Airport two years ago. He is a different boy than the one who sat in the high school cafeteria eating his lunch facing the wall so that he wouldn't have to make eye contact with the other students. During the months that followed Nhi's stay in Arlington Hospital, we have learned a great deal about the heavy burden of fear and low self-esteem which he carried with him from Vietnam. And although it took some time for us to integrate this new knowledge into our daily lives, Nhi's attempt to take his life has become a watershed in our understanding of each other and in Nhi's own understanding of himself.

Nhi's new self-respect is reflected in his ability to reach out to others, especially newly arrived students struggling with English and handicapped students trying to come to terms with their lot in life. At Washington-Lee High School, Nhi has become a special friend to Bich Ngoc, a Vietnamese girl who is blind. And recently Debi overheard Nhi giving a pep talk to a young Vietnamese student with severely limited hearing. The boy's family was discouraging him from trying to get an education.

"You can do anything! That's the first thing you have to understand," Nhi said. "The problem with your family is that just because you're handicapped, they think you're helpless. They think that because you have a physical problem, you must have a brain problem too. That's not true! Having weak ears doesn't make you stupid. You're smart.

"For sixteen years my aunt and uncle told me not to

worry because they would take care of me. I thought I couldn't take care of myself. But I can. And you can too!"

Nhi's friend was puzzled by his words and did not fully comprehend this message of freedom. The effects of years of self-doubt and dependence could not be overcome by Nhi's simple exhortations—or even his example. But Nhi persisted in sharing his exciting hope of self-fulfillment and independence. One day he even roped Debi in to back up his claims. He gave a lengthy lecture to his friend in Vietnamese, and then turned expectantly to Debi. "Right, Mom?" It took them all a few moments to realize there was a language barrier.

Within a few months after he got out of the hospital, Nhi was an active swimmer. Every morning at 6:00 A.M. the boy we couldn't get out of bed walked to the high school pool to join retired folks for an "early bird swim." In the locker room, he removed his braces and crutches and then wheeled himself to the edge of the pool. There he climbed down the ladder, and wearing a flotation swimsuit to hold up his hips, he swam laps. Once in the pool, Nhi felt a freedom that he never experienced on land. He propelled himself easily through the water with his powerful shoulders and arms.

After his laps, he showered and chatted or sang hymns with the older men in the locker room. Sometimes he entertained them with songs on his harmonica. It wasn't the traditional high school locker room experience, but for Nhi it provided a warm atmosphere of shared accomplishment and friendship.

At the end of his sophomore year, Debi and I told Nhi that we wanted him to sign up for summer driver's education classes at the school. Nhi looked very serious. "Mom, Dad, I have something to tell you," he said earnestly. "I don't think my legs are strong enough for me to drive a car." Debi and I suppressed a smile. We explained to Nhi how many people who don't have the use of their legs are able to drive with hand controls. Nhi was elated to learn that we had already looked into getting hand controls for our car.

Driving provided Nhi with another boost to his growing

self-confidence and independence. Behind the wheel, he was no longer limping along in back of his peers, but clearly an equal. He began to blossom in unexpected ways and he changed from being a loner and follower to being a leader.

In the winter of his junior year he decided to form a band with other Vietnamese boys to play at the school's International Night, and he even convinced his hard-of-hearing friend to join the group. The other boys had more difficulty with English than Nhi, and they were reluctant to ask a teacher to sponsor them or find a room in which to practice. "I have to do all the work," Nhi complained one evening. "I don't know why no one else can do it. They just depend on me to get everything done." He couldn't hide the note of pride in his voice from his equally proud parents.

I was pleased to see Nhi beginning to feel more comfortable with other Vietnamese people. His new self-confidence was enabling him to overcome barriers and misconceptions, and the International Night was a big success. Nhi's band played a medley of songs from around the world to a packed high school auditorium. Nhi himself played the harmonica and sang and directed. My parents were there, and friends from the church, and I marveled at all the students who shared not only their talents, but the music and dance from their native countries as well. It made me proud to be an American to know that while many of the students came from war-torn countries, they were able to celebrate peace and freedom with us in the United States.

Occasionally there were sad reminders of the obstacles that still confronted Nhi. One beautiful spring afternoon, when the cherry blossoms were in full bloom, Debi and I took the boys to the Jefferson Memorial for a walk around the Tidal Basin. We walked hand in hand while Hy pushed Nhi ten yards ahead of us.

Halfway through our walk we passed by a small group of Vietnamese teenagers. Nhi and Hy were well ahead of us when one of the girls turned to the other and in our hearing said "que" (pronounced quay). Both girls laughed scornfully. It was a derogatory Vietnamese word sometimes used to describe handicapped people and it implied "leech" or "heavy burden." I turned and scowled at the girls, and one of them hastened to reassure me, "I'm not talking about you. I'm talking about him!" She pointed ahead to Nhi.

I felt angry and depressed. Nothing I could say or do would make these attractive, well-educated young girls see my son as a human being deserving of respect and admiration. I wondered how Nhi had survived a lifetime of such abuse. The only consolation was that Nhi was talking happily with Hy and walking too far ahead to have overheard our conversation.

By the end of his junior year, Nhi was even more independent. He worked as a registrar at a local pool and made many new friends. He spent much of his money for evening entertainment (as we learned later, much to our chagrin!), but was able to save some to send to his aunt and uncle in Saigon. Sometimes Nhi and Hy also sent small packages of cloth, pens, after-shave lotion, and toys which they said their aunt and uncle could sell on the market. Several Vietnamese businessmen had set up shop in our Arlington neighborhood for flying packages to Vietnam, and although the service was expensive, it was fairly reliable. When the goods arrived in Saigon, the recipients received a notice from the airport. They then stood in line for twelve or more hours, waiting to pass through customs. A heavy tax was applied to all packages, but Nhi's and Hy's aunt and uncle were still able to make a profit on the resale of the items they received. In this way they were able to supplement their income.

Debi and I were still puzzled by Nhi's and Hy's strange attitude toward their aunt and uncle. On one hand they seemed to be devoted nephews; on the other hand letters and pictures from Vietnam inevitably made them quiet and withdrawn, even depressed. Something clearly was wrong, but we were unable to find out what.

I thought perhaps for Nhi the problem was that his aunt and uncle still saw him as "Little Nhi" who was unable to take care of himself. It was clear that Nhi took great satisfaction and pride in providing financially for his aunt and uncle, but because they didn't expect him to work, they never understood that he contributed to the gifts. While their aunt and uncle wrote Hy about his schooling and career plans, they rarely discussed these topics with Nhi. They continued to use the diminutive in reference to Nhi, and mostly inquired after his health.

"They still think I'm a little boy," Nhi explained. "It's hard for them to imagine that I am now a man. When they come to America, they will understand that I am no longer 'Little Nhi,' but I have grown up. My aunt and uncle know a lot about loving and caring for children in Vietnam, but they do not understand about the world outside, especially here in America."

Nhi was right. He had changed dramatically, and if his aunt and uncle ever escaped from Vietnam they would be shocked to see the changes in him—and in Hy. Hy has been academically very successful, maintaining an A average in his high school courses. He is sometimes like a machine—driven to do better and better, and I have to *order* him to go outside and play some basketball or soccer.

Hy is also changing spiritually. He is full of questions after Gordon's sermons on Sunday, and he has begun to read his Bible. "From Buddha, I learned a lot of ideas about living a good life," he once said. "But I didn't learn about love and forgiveness. Of course," he hastily added, "Buddha did say it is better to eat vegetables given with love than meat given with hatred."

At church we usually sit in the front row so that Nhi will not have to walk any farther than necessary. It is a joyful experience to worship with the people who made our family possible. After each service, the members often greet us and say what a blessing it is to have the four of us with them. It *is* a gift. By accepting God's call to become instant parents at the age of twenty-six, Debi and I have been blessed beyond measure, with blessings "pressed down, shaken together, and flowing over."

My only frustration, if it can be called that, is trying to get Nhi and Hy to assert themselves more. They defer to Debi and me for everything, even on such simple questions as to which movies they want to see. "You decide, Dad," they always say. "You know best." I admit I get little sympathy from other friends with teenagers when I complain about this deference! But sometimes things seem a bit too perfect. Despite the emotional trauma of Nhi's back operation and his attempted suicide, the rest of our time together as a family has been a great joy. My own experiences growing up in a family of five boys had many more "down" times than we have experienced. Whatever the future holds, it is a comfort to know that our family relationships are solid, and we have many dreams left to share.

20
HY

Beyond Dale Carnegie

The night Nhi drank the drain cleaner, I felt angry and afraid. If Nhi died, I would have no purpose for living. I knew I was wrong to follow Mom and Dad when they told me to stop helping him, and I was angry at them for pushing Nhi to do so many things. I too had been selfish. In only taking care of myself, I had forgotten the promise I made to Ma and Ba before leaving Vietnam. It was my duty to care for my older brother Nhi.

I remembered a sad day in Vietnam. Our family was living in a small village, and there was a big festival. One young man told his sister she could not attend. She went anyway, and when her brother caught her there, he beat her. He had beaten her many times before, but this time she was so embarrassed she drank poison, and she died.

After she died, I went to see the coffin. The house was so crowded with people I had trouble getting in the door. I could not see the brother anywhere. I asked someone standing nearby where the brother of the dead woman had gone, and he pointed toward the coffin. "Underneath," he said. The brother was crouched there, silent and lonely. I pitied his situation. But I thought he deserved his sadness because he caused his sister's suicide.

I did not want to be like that brother. After Nhi came home from the hospital I made a solemn promise to love him more. He would never feel neglected again; I would do everything possible for him. I began to wait on him just as I had done in Vietnam. I was as good as I could be.

For a few weeks, everything went fine. In the morning, Nhi and I ate breakfast together—Chinese noodles with

fish sauce. Then I carried him downstairs and pushed him
to school in his wheelchair. In the afternoons, I pushed him
home again, and carried him up the stairs to our house.

Then something happened. Nhi changed. He started to
get up by himself and fix breakfast. He walked up and down
the stairs with his braces and crutches, and when I tried
to help him, he pushed me away. He didn't say anything,
but I knew what he meant. He no longer wanted my help.
We didn't argue or disagree, because that is not the Vietnamese way. We kept our problems inside of us, and I did
not know what to do.

At school, I started to do my own things and Nhi did
his. I did not even want to look at him when we passed
each other in the hallway, and we did not speak. Why did
he now push his own wheelchair? That was my job too.

Before long, Nhi had many new friends, and he started
to stay after school to visit with them. I didn't have many
friends so I came home by myself and started my homework.
While I was at my desk, I could hear Nhi walk up the stairs.
It made me feel sad and depressed. Before he learned to
walk, and again when he was in his cast, it had been my
job to carry him up the stairs. I wished I could take Nhi's
crutches away and throw him on my back again.

Nhi and I didn't talk as much at home as we used to.
Mom and Dad joked about that. It was so embarrassing.
But I always knew how Nhi felt and he knew how I felt
without talking. Mom and Dad started to push me more
than they pushed Nhi, and they seemed more at ease with
him than they were with me.

I started to feel very lonely. At school it was hard to
make friends with American students. Often I dreamed
about my best friend who was still in Vietnam. I wished I
could share my worries and problems with him. One time
I did have a crush on a Vietnamese girl in my class. But
she was too Americanized to like a Vietnamese guy.

I developed a written daily schedule and became very
strict with myself. I was a perfectionist. I wanted people
to see me as a serious student and to like me. My time
was always devoted to my studies. Sometimes I was irritable,
and I was always quiet. I began to long for the day when

I would return to Vietnam as a doctor. I missed the scenes and joyful sounds of little children running naked in the streets, happy in a tropical rain storm. I missed the fishing boats, and the neighbors calling a greeting to one another, or giving away some precious food. I never saw these things in America.

At the end of my junior year, I started to read some Dale Carnegie books on how to make friends. I learned how to make jokes and say the right thing. For instance, people at the Church of the Saviour sometimes asked me what my religion was. I always answered, "Buddhist and Christian." I was really a Buddhist, but I thought I should say what people wanted to hear. It would make them feel more comfortable and they would like me better. I got that idea from reading Dale Carnegie.

One day, in the summer, while we were at the beach, Dad got angry at me for reading those books. He said I was not being myself, and I would have more friends if I just acted naturally. But I knew he was wrong. When I acted like myself, I had no friends. It was only when I was not myself that people liked me.

Mom said it would get easier to make American friends when I got older. She said sometimes it is hard for American teenagers to get to know people who are different from them. I would have more friends when I got to college. That was a year away and I didn't know if I could wait that long.

Then Dad suggested that I read the Bible. Because I was searching for ways to make myself a better person, I followed his suggestion. I saw the Bible as a self-improvement book that would help me make friends and have people like me. But I was surprised when I began to read the Sermon on the Mount in the fifth chapter of Matthew. The words struck me so hard. I learned about the wonderful person named Jesus. He was so humble and so powerful that when he said, "Follow me," I had to follow him. His words were too solid and concrete for me to ignore.

I raced through the rest of the Gospels to find out more about this man. There was no doubt in my mind that Jesus was God when I read the other Gospels. I also read *Seeds of Contemplation* by Thomas Merton. This helped me to understand how truly bold was Jesus' teaching.

For some time I felt a great sense of peace. I had left Dale Carnegie to follow Jesus, and because for sixteen years of my life I always believed what others said without questioning them, I embarked on the Christian life wholeheartedly. I took notes on the New Testament and tried to do what Jesus taught. I also began to study Buddhism. At the time of my conversion to Christianity, I had little true knowledge of Buddhism; I had never thought about it for myself, but merely followed what my parents taught me. Now I found that there was much that was good in Buddhism because of its emphasis on living a good life, taking care of the poor, and being kind to one's neighbor. Spiritual growth depended upon one's relationship to others and life's difficulties were not to be questioned, but accepted. But in Buddhism there was no personal relationship with God, and no grace. It was a relief to know that I did not have to work hard all my life and still not know if I would be reincarnated as a better person. Because of Jesus' sacrifice, I could become like Him and one day live with God forever.

There was something else very big that happened during this time. Mom started writing a book about our family. She asked me many questions about our life in Vietnam. Nhi and I had carefully agreed on what to tell Mom and Dad about our family. But Mom asked such good questions, ones we had never thought of before. Each time we talked, I quickly told Nhi what I had said so that Mom would hear the same stories from both of us. But the questions kept coming. I wondered how Mom got all her ideas for those questions.

Although we had been in America for three years, Nhi still had nightmares about being sent back to Vietnam. Sometimes I desperately wanted to tell Mom and Dad the truth, but when I saw how afraid Nhi was I remained quiet. Also, neither one of us wanted to hurt Mom and Dad with the truth. Mom had so much feeling of being our mother, we knew that she would feel she had lost her children if she found out our Vietnamese parents were still alive. We wanted to protect her from those hurt feelings.

Sometimes I thought about how strange our life of secrets had become. When I left Vietnam I thought it would be great to escape the conflicts of the teenage years with Ma and Ba. I never thought about having conflicts with my new American parents. But the lie was such a heavy burden that it made me feel nervous around Mom and Dad. I always tried to be exceptionally good so that they would never get angry with me and send me back to Vietnam. But I could never know for sure what might happen.

When Mom's questions kept coming, Nhi and I made up a new story. We decided that if Mom asked us any more about our parents, we would say that we had two sets of aunts and uncles instead of just one. That would explain the things that didn't fit in our story of being raised by only one aunt and uncle after our parents died. We waited for a good time to tell the new story.

Sometimes the weight of all these lies seemed too much. I wanted to get rid of them. But at other times I felt like Nhi. He thought that our stories had much truth in them. We would never see our parents again. So in many ways we were orphans, and we were thankful that we had a new mother and father to take care of us.

21
DEBI

A Baffling Mystery

Ever since Hy and Nhi had arrived, Steve and I had wondered if someday we should write a book to share the joys
and sorrows of our international family. I had kept a journal
of many of the poignant or humorous things the boys had
said. When we showed our refugee camp slides to churches
and schools, the reception was always warm, and many people asked us to write a book about our experiences. We
received the same response when we published an article
in the *Washington Post* about our first three years together.

During the boys' junior year, I began to interview them
about their life in Vietnam. We taped their answers, and
Nhi and Hy both enjoyed speaking into the microphone.
Their stories were fascinating, and I was moved by all that
they had seen and suffered during their early years. It was
one thing to read about the Vietnam war in newspapers
and books; it was quite another to hear one's own children
speak earnestly of their firsthand experiences. As one who
had become their mother later in their lives, I was grateful
for an opportunity to fill in the missing years. I felt that I
was getting to know them better and better, and my sense
of maternal attachment grew daily.

The longer we talked, however, the more puzzled I became. There were several small discrepancies in Nhi's and
Hy's story. They had pictures of their aunt and uncle, but
no pictures of their parents. They never celebrated their
parent's "Death Day," although that was an important Buddhist tradition to insure a better afterlife for ancestors. Although nine of their aunt's and uncle's children were now
in the U.S., and Nhi and Hy had lived with them for many

years, they were never in contact with any of their cousins and didn't even know where they lived.

These things, coupled with the boys' sad reaction to letters from Vietnam, made me wonder if there was some deep mystery surrounding the relationship with their aunt and uncle. Nhi and Hy had always been honest with us, so I was certain there was some logical explanation to my questions. Were they trying to cover up for some private family sadness?

One evening, when Hy was at Boys State, I sat down with Steve and showed him my list of questions. Steve was equally puzzled, and called Nhi downstairs to talk with us. Nhi wanted to wait until Hy got home, but when we questioned him further, he explained that he and Hy had two sets of aunts and uncles, one of which was poor, one of which was rich. In order to make us think that they came from a rich family, they had told us only about their wealthy aunt and uncle, although they had lived with their poor aunt and uncle.

When we went to bed that evening, Steve had an unsettling explanation for Nhi's story. "The aunt and uncle are their mother and father," he said matter-of-factly. "Their parents are still alive, and that's who they lived with until they left Vietnam."

I was shocked that Steve could even think such a thing. However, Nhi's explanations raised more questions than they answered, and we seemed farther from the truth than ever. Just as I was beginning to think that I really understood my sons, here was the most baffling mystery of all. Would we ever really know them?

22
HY

Will You Still Love Me?

I was surprised when Mom and Dad picked me up at the American Legion post when I got back from Boys State. I knew they were planning to be on a church retreat, and I was worried that something had happened to Nhi. "Is Nhi okay?" I asked over and over again. Mom and Dad said he was home cooking Vietnamese food, but I wasn't convinced. They looked so serious. I tried very hard to cheer them up, but they did not cooperate.

The three of us drove to a sandwich shop and sat at a table in an empty corner. Dad looked very serious while we ate. Then he looked straight at me and said, "This week, Nhi told us that some of the stories you and he told us about your life in Vietnam were not true. Mom and I wondered if you would also like to make a few corrections."

I was so afraid that I didn't say anything. What had Nhi told them? Dad reminded me that he and Mom had still wanted to be a family with Nhi and me even after they learned that we had lied about our ages. But he refused to tell me what Nhi had said while I was gone.

I had to figure out whether Nhi had told them the truth or the story about two aunts and two uncles. I looked at Mom and Dad. I could not guess. So I told them the new story, about the aunts and uncles. Dad said he did not believe me. Mom said the most important thing was not what my story was, but that I tell the truth.

Tears started to stream down my face. The moment I had feared for three years had arrived. Would I really be able to take care of Nhi and me by myself? And how would Ma and Ba feel if we were forced to return to Vietnam? Their dream for a new life for their sons would be over.

The neighbors would laugh at us. Our family would never come to America, and the new house I planned to buy for Ma would never be.

"Dad, I have sinned. Please take me to a church," I sobbed.

"No, Hy. I want you to tell us the truth," he answered.

"My parents are not dead," I said, afraid to look at Mom and Dad. "They are still in Vietnam. A younger brother and sister live with them. Another sister died when she was three years old."

Mom explained to me that she and Dad were not sad that my parents were alive. They were very glad. "But we are hurt that for three years you have not told us the truth. Trust is a big part of love and we haven't had trust in our relationship."

I kept sobbing. "Will you still love me? Will you still be my parents?"

Mom took my hand. "We still love you, Hy, and we want you to be our son."

I couldn't believe it. "Really?"

"Yes," Dad said. "We still want to be a family and to be your American parents."

Mom said that although there was a big hole in our family's relationship where there should have been trust, we could start right then, and be honest with one another. We had many good times and lots of love together. We could build on that.

I was amazed that Mom and Dad still loved me, and wanted me to live with them. I thought they would be so ashamed to tell their neighbors about the lie that they would kick us out. But I had something else to confess.

"I also lied when I said we lived in a nice house in Saigon. It was a poor house, without a shower or any of the nice things I said. We were embarrassed for you to know that our family was poor."

Mom said that she and Dad did not love us any more or less because of how much money our family had. She said they didn't go to the refugee camp to live with rich people, and they sponsored us because that is what they heard God telling them to do.

Dad asked me if it made me angry that he and Mom

had so much more than my family in Vietnam. He said it probably didn't seem fair, and it wasn't fair. I told him that I hated rich people in Vietnam, because they sucked from the poor, but I did not hate him. I explained that when I first came to America, I thought I could get friends by being rich and giving people lots of food. I always fixed a big snack for anyone who came to our house. But then I realized that money and food did not make friends.

It made me happy when Dad said he believed I was telling the truth. "You have been an honest person in every other way," he said. "I imagine it feels good to get this burden off your shoulders." He said he understood how fear paralyzed me from telling the truth.

I told Mom and Dad how many times before I wanted to tell them, but was too afraid. I explained how I always hated saying my parents were killed. In order to be believable, I always had to say "dead" or "killed" with feeling. But I worried that if I said it too strongly, I might make it come true.

"Starting this night, I am always going to tell the truth," I promised. Mom explained that they did not tell me what Nhi had said because they felt it was important for me to tell the truth myself. Nhi and Mom and Dad had already talked everything over and prayed together.

Mom and Dad put their arms around me as we walked to the car. In a few minutes we were home. Nhi was there cooking spring rolls for Father's Day and he saw by our happy faces that everything had turned out all right.

Dad went to the office while Mom and I kept talking. I told her about Boys State and how some of the guys didn't like me because I was Vietnamese. But then others wanted to know about my escape from Vietnam. They asked me why some Vietnamese didn't like to talk about their lives before they came to America. I told them that many people have memories that are too painful to discuss.

When I was standing in the cafeteria line one day, another boy asked me for an example of how life in Vietnam was difficult. I told him about the time I had to stand in line for our family's food ration from the communist government. After half of the people in line got their food, the government ran out. I returned home empty handed. And I knew that meant my family's stomachs would be empty too.

I told Mom all about Boys State and then I showed her pictures of my family that I had kept hidden in my room. In one picture, we were all standing in front of our house which was surrounded by sandbags to protect us from bullets and other things that explode. There was a picture of my sister, who we used to tease by calling her "Ba Dia chu"—*landowner*—because she had fat cheeks and looked so serious and greedy. In another picture, my younger brother was wearing a shirt and tie that Ma made from a piece of material Mom sent them from America. Just that night Mom was wearing a skirt made from the same material, and we laughed about it. It made me feel that my two families were connected.

"Mom," I said, "when my Vietnamese mother comes to America, I hope you will be like Vietnamese neighbors to each other. In Vietnam, 'neighbor' has a special meaning. Neighbors help each other, and lend things, and discuss problems together."

I also told my Mom that now I knew she and Dad really loved us. "And when you get old, I will take care of you. I will set a good example for my children by the way I take care of my parents."

Mom and I talked until 2:00 a.m. Mom gave me a hug, and said she loved me. Mom had stopped hugging me and kissing me good night a long time ago, when she realized that I didn't like it very much. "Mom, I haven't had a hug in almost two years. I love you, too. And this time I really mean it." I gave her a kiss and said good night.

23
DEBI

A *Deeper Bond*

I pulled into the hospital parking lot and walked to the surgical waiting room. Nhi was having an operation on his wrist to replace a dying bone with a silicone rubber bone. He had injured it in a fall while walking to school. The surgeon had said Nhi needed surgery as soon as possible or other bones in his arm would move into the empty space.

In some ways it seemed like all the other times that I had gone to the hospital for Nhi, but this time was different. I checked in with the Red Cross Volunteer at the desk, and told her why I was there.

She found Nhi's name on her list. "And what is your relationship to the patient?"

It seemed like such a simple question. For three years I had answered that question without hesitation. "Mother." It had been several weeks since I learned Nhi's parents were still alive, and it was the first time I was forced to think about the terminology of our new relationship. I cleared my throat. The woman looked at me, perhaps surprised by my slow response to her question. How could I say "Mother" anymore? I was not a mother in the way I had assumed.

"Foster mother," I replied with some embarrassment.

"Oh, how sweet of you to be a foster parent. I think that's just wonderful. How do you like the boy you're taking care of?"

I immediately regretted saying I was a foster mother. From the woman's question I could tell she thought I was only temporarily taking care of another woman's child, and I wanted to explain to her how for three years I thought

146

I was Nhi's mother. I had cared for him, and nursed him through two hospitalizations. We had even had some of the same "bonding" that takes place between younger children and their parents. We had taught our sons how to speak English, helped Nhi learn to walk, rejoiced over his first faltering steps, and introduced both boys to the joys and mysteries of a whole new culture.

The woman was still waiting for my answer. "Yes," I replied. "I like the boy very much."

"That's great! It's such a wonderful thing you are doing. Your doctor is very good about talking with parents after operations, and I know he will come to see you as soon as he can."

I took a seat and thumbed through a book about refugees in Latin America and Vietnam. The stories did not give me the same challenged feeling I normally received reading about other people's trouble. I was feeling betrayed and confused.

I had really meant it when I told the boys I was glad their parents were still alive, and that we would still be their American family. But in the days following the revelation that they were not orphans, I found myself feeling more and more resentful. I thought of all the sleepless nights I had spent by Nhi's side, the hours of physical therapy, and the sidestep from the partnership track at work. And more than time and money, there was my deep emotional commitment. I had given of myself to Nhi and Hy in a way which they had not returned. I had trusted them, but for three years they had not trusted us enough to tell us the truth about who they were and where they were from. If I had not started writing a book, we probably never would have learned the truth.

I wondered if Nhi and Hy were secretly laughing at Steve and me for the time and money we had spent on them. I suspected that the whole Vietnamese community was in on the deception. Few of them had ever referred to Nhi and Hy as our sons. "The two boys you take care of," is what the Vietnamese we knew had called them. Did everyone but us know all along that we weren't parents?

Now that I knew the truth, I was having a hard time

getting my work on the book done. *My story keeps inter-rupting my story,* I mused. *Which story am I writing? How many stories will I write and find out later that they are false? And do I even have a story anymore?*

The surgeon and his resident interrupted my resentful thoughts. The operation had gone well, but they would not be able to put a cast on Nhi's wrist for at least twelve days. Until then he would not be allowed to put any weight on it. With only one limb left to use, he would be unable to walk or even propel his own wheelchair.

The surgeon asked me how I met Nhi and Hy and if their parents were dead. I explained that their mother and father were still living in Vietnam. "Oh," he said. "So you are taking care of the boys until their parents come!"

Again, I felt a need to convey the depth of my commit-ment to Nhi and Hy. The doctor's version sounded like I was babysitting until their parents arrived. I wasn't a baby-sitter, I was a mother! I wanted to protest. I was angry at myself for even caring that two strangers understand our complex relationship. But I also knew the problem was more than that—it was that I no longer understood our relationship.

During the next two weeks, Nhi required a great deal of care. I had to perform many times one of the same diffi-cult tasks I had done joyfully in the past—lifting him and his wheelchair down the sidewalk to the street. Now I found myself resenting Nhi's physical needs and the way they disrupted my schedule. Sometimes after carrying him I secretly cried. They were tears of anger, frustration, and pain.

What hurt me the most was Nhi's and Hy's explanation for keeping their secret. They had been afraid we would kick them out of the house. I wanted to ask them how they could think that after all we had been through to-gether. What more would they need to understand how much we loved them?

I consoled myself with the thought that since Steve had made it quite clear we would still be a family, Nhi and Hy would at last come to love and trust us. I breathed a sigh of relief and looked forward to more meaningful relationships as the summer progressed.

Instead, the summer months were a time of additional strain. We had been through many hard times *together*, but now it seemed as if each one of us needed to go our separate ways. Nhi and Hy both seemed increasingly withdrawn emotionally. Hy spent long hours in his room reading with his door shut while Nhi stayed out late at night with a new group of friends. From their point of view, family life seemed to be over. Try as we might to become a family, they were convinced it would never work now that Steve and I knew their parents were still alive.

Their aloofness played on my own wounds. Just as Nhi and Hy needed ever stronger assurances of my love and commitment, I found that I too was withdrawing. My hurt and anger prevented me from seeing clearly the motivation for their deception, and I felt a need to have healing of my own before I could offer healing to my "sons."

Over the course of the summer, I did heal. I wrote a letter to Nhi's and Hy's mother. I had written her for three years as "aunt"; I was concerned that she might worry about what would happen to Nhi and Hy now that the truth was out. I assured her that Steve and I still loved her sons and that we would continue to take care of them until she was able to emigrate to America.

Nhi's and Hy's mother wrote a beautiful reply. She thanked me, as she had done in previous letters, for all that we had done. She concluded by saying that she had no intention of ever taking Nhi and Hy away from me. "We are both their mothers," she explained.

It wasn't long before I knew that she was right. During Nhi's and Hy's early years, she was their only mother. But during their last three years, we had shared their mothering, she from afar and I in person. Because of her incredible love for them, I became a mother to two whole, healthy teenaged boys. I was deeply grateful for the love their biological mother gave and continued to give. Perhaps in the future when she came to America we would share mothering in a more direct way.

With my own hurt healed, I was able to understand Nhi's
and Hy's position better. I knew that it was unlikely I would
have acted differently had I been in their shoes. Hy thought
if he could just get his brother to America, then the doctors
would fix his legs. The boys trusted an older, "wiser" relative
who to their eyes knew a great deal about America. His
advice to reduce their ages and say their parents were dead
seemed eminently sensible if Americans would not sponsor
them otherwise. (Ironically, Steve and I had briefly considered sponsoring a family of four from the Songkhla Children's Center who told us their parents were still in Saigon.
In response to God's call we would have sponsored Nhi
and Hy even if we had known that they were not orphans.)

Nhi and Hy had also grown up in a society where deception was necessary to insure survival. No one knew for sure
who was a member of the Viet Cong or who supported
the Saigon government. Secret papers and false travel docu-
ments were the norm, and no one was to be trusted. Anyone
could be a secret communist.

After the communist victory in 1975, people developed
another way of survival. To escape the concentration camps,
men lied about their former occupations. Teenaged boys
hid in the forest to avoid being sent to fight in occupied
Cambodia. False papers protected Nhi and Hy even as they
traveled by bus to the boat that took them to Thailand.

After years of war and communist rule, Nhi and Hy suddenly found themselves in a society operating on radically
different principles. There were no secret police and no
spies waiting to turn them in for speaking the wrong political doctrine. In spite of their inflated view of the CIA, there
was no one who would ever uncover their secret. They
were now part of a society that worked largely on trust
and disclosure. The truth ethic was so powerful that a President was forced to resign, not for ordering a break-in, but
for lying about it after it had taken place.

Nhi and Hy had much to cope with upon their arrival
in America. There was the grief of losing their family and
country, the disappointment that doctors were unable to
cure Nhi's paralysis, and the strange language and customs.
To their surprise, there were also American parents who

loved them and treated them like "real" sons. They had been worried that they might be treated poorly, like the sad "chan bo"—cowherd—whose tattered rags and hungry eyes they both remembered well. Now they discovered that two perfect strangers were ready to adopt them.

For Steve and me, our relationship with Nhi and Hy was straightforward and joyous. We knew our own hearts and our commitment to them, and we also knew much more about them than they did about us. For their part, they were two vulnerable, dependent boys suddenly thrown in with perfect strangers whom they had no reason to trust. Anything might happen, and their past had taught them that at any given moment, a new tragedy was just around the corner.

As the months had passed and Nhi and Hy had seen that our love was lasting and genuine, they had had a new burden to bear. Although at their first Christmas they were delighted with the presents they received, by the next year they were deeply worried about how they would ever repay us for our gifts. They also were beginning to understand how hurt we would be if we learned that they had not been honest with us. They had no one with whom to share their anxiety and confusion. Their fear paralyzed them, and made it impossible for them to trust any friends with their secret. The longer they waited to tell us, the more difficult it became to extricate themselves from the lie.

I learned from Nhi that he had come to think of himself as an orphan, and he really did view us as his true parents. I remembered a story I had read about a young Jewish girl in Poland during World War II. To save her life, the child had posed as the niece of a Catholic family. As time went on, she actually came to believe that she was both Catholic and a niece. Had she only been acting her part, she might have given herself away. By becoming her part, and denying for a time her true heritage, she survived the Holocaust. Her response seemed both reasonable and compelling.

With all these thoughts, I found myself opening up again to Nhi and Hy. They in turn began to communicate their own fears and hurts. We were forced to verbalize more

clearly our love and commitment to one another, and we
renewed our promise to stand by our family. Nhi and Hy
came to understand that while Ma and Ba were their Vietnamese parents, we were their American parents. Having
weathered this most recent storm, Steve and I felt more
bonded to them than ever. For the first time, we felt like
we really knew our sons and they knew us. And we realized
that we were committed to Nhi and Hy for life—whatever
our individual or family future might bring.

Epilogue
DEBI

Nhi and Hy graduated from Washington-Lee High School in June of 1984. Hy was a valedictorian of his class and one of the first to receive his diploma. Nhi was at the end, on crutches, hoping no one would bump him. An hour before the ceremony, there had been a sudden downpour. The ground was muddy and the ramp to the speakers' stand was wet and slippery.

Steve and I sat in the outdoor bleachers with his parents and brother, and dozens of friends from our church and neighborhood. As Nhi started up the ramp, I thought back to the three years before when he had walked forward in the gym to receive his English award. So much had happened since then. The operations, learning to walk, telling the truth about his parents, normal teenage rebellion. Then there was Nhi's acceptance to St. Andrews Presbyterian College and Hy's acceptance at the University of Virginia. It was a big step for both boys to go to separate colleges, and I wondered how they would adjust.

Once again, I felt like the boys' mother. I realized even more how parenting is a function of accepted responsibility, not biology. I did not know how things would be when Ma and Ba came to America, but we had already weathered so much, I was certain we would be able to work that through as well.

Now Nhi was slowly walking up the ramp to the stage. He moved carefully, at an angle, and the graduates clapped and leapt to their feet. Soon the entire audience joined them. Steve and I hugged one another and our friends, while Nhi gracefully received his diploma and walked back to his seat.

Today Hy is a pre-med student at the University of Virginia. He hopes one day to be a doctor serving low-income people, perhaps in Washington, D.C. or Vietnam. He is a volunteer at a mental health center in Charlottesville, and a paid translator for a Vietnamese patient.

Nhi is studying computer science and plans to stay in his adopted country after graduation. Although he would like to visit Vietnam some day, the prevailing prejudice against handicapped people prevents him from ever wanting to live there.

When Nhi first went to college, he was extremely lonely. Later he told us that as he watched me drive away on the first day, he felt as if he were back in Vietnam, being left behind at the orphanage. "I just had to find a way to get back home," he said.

Since then, Nhi has made tremendous progress in living on his own. He even went to Hawaii with a group of students for the winter term. During his Christmas vacation, Steve teased Nhi about his past reluctance to help in family chores. He wanted to know if Nhi was going to help out at home again or if work would make him feel like a "cowherd" servant instead of a "real son." Nhi laughed, but then became very serious. "There is another kind of adoptive parents," he said. "That's the kind that doesn't abuse you or spoil you, but teaches you how to deal with problems and the real world. That's the kind I like, and that's the kind you are." It was one of the best compliments we ever received.

Epilogue
NHI

A few weeks after the start of my freshman year, I was rolling my wheelchair across a bridge over a lake. I stopped in the middle and laughed. Not many years ago, I had never even dreamed I could go to college. Only last year, the thought made me very afraid. Now I laughed because I was so proud of myself.

If I had stayed in Vietnam, my life would have been a prison. I would have stayed home forever, helping my parents in their little store. I would always worry about who would take care of me, whether there would be enough food, and how I would get to the bathroom. Education would have been out of the question, and I would be very shy and quiet, not aggressive like I am now.

I thank God for the chance he has given me to change, and for making me who I am now. My world view has become much larger. I can talk to people on my own, and do everything for myself. Even when no one is around to push me, I can make it on my own.

Until a few years ago, I never thought I could make other people happy and make them feel good. But now I know that when I try to do things that are difficult for me, other people are encouraged. Last summer a middle-aged woman told me that watching me swim gave her courage to take swimming lessons for the first time. She figured if I could do it with only my arms, she could do it with arms *and* legs.

Sometimes when I don't care about other people, I think of all the people who cared for me. And then I want to help anyone I can. I think I help other handicapped people by keeping a happy face, by not being mad at the world or making trouble. Then when people look at me, they realize that handicapped people can do many things. It is a privilege to help others think well of handicapped people.

Even though I sit in a wheelchair and walk with crutches, I want to be like other people. I don't want to be left out, and it makes me happy when people don't turn away from me. Then I don't feel as if I have lost something. Perhaps because I am friendly, many people feel comfortable talking to me. My friends are boys and girls, men and women, blacks, whites, Hispanics, and Vietnamese. Sometimes guys who act "tough" to others are gentle with me.

Before I had friends, I always felt sorry for myself. Now I feel special. I wonder if I would be a different person if I could walk. My personality might make me a wild guy. But because of polio, I think more about what I should do, and what my limitations and abilities are. I am a kinder person. Perhaps it is better for me to be handicapped.

Wherever I go I think a lot about my American Mom and Dad. They have taught me to be independent and given me courage. But I am glad to know that there is someone I can hold on to, and call in case of trouble.

Recently at school we had a dance for handicapped students. When I arrived, everyone was sitting on the sides of the room. I danced with one girl for a few minutes and then introduced her to another guy. While they danced together, I asked another girl to dance. Then I found her a partner, and I kept on asking girls to dance until soon everyone was on the floor having fun. It was so different from the first party I went to here in America. There a beautiful girl asked me to dance and I refused because I thought everyone would laugh at me. Now I am too happy to worry about that anymore.

Epilogue
HY

In the past few years almost all my dreams have come true. Some of these dreams were very big and some seem small compared to the material wealth which is found in America. I have escaped from Vietnam. I have American parents who love me. I am attending a university, and I can eat a whole piece of chicken and drink an entire Coke at dinner.

There has been both gain and loss in coming to America. I no longer think and act the way I did in Vietnam. But I do not want to forsake my Vietnamese culture and become totally assimilated into American culture. To choose one or the other—Vietnam or America—might be easier. But I want to be bicultural. As a result, I am not completely at ease in either culture, but I have absorbed some of the richness of each.

During the last four years, living with Mom and Dad has taught me to feel comfortable with Americans. I have learned to socialize with them, discuss religious and political issues, and ask for assistance when I need it. I have gained a great deal of confidence and security from watching the way that Mom and Dad are bold with others. They have taught me that in the American system I can boldly ask for help and interact with others in a businesslike manner. My friends who have just come from Vietnam often don't realize this, so I explain to them that it is all right to take initiative in America.

I value and have learned to embrace the freedom of questioning beliefs of those who are older than I. These Americans, unlike many Vietnamese adults, will answer my questions instead of thinking I am impolite to ask them.

And Mom and Dad have shown me how to disagree with others without becoming angry or wanting to fight. In Vietnam, I was always afraid to disagree with people because I thought it would make them want to fight me. Now I value the freedom to express my ideas more freely. I can talk about events openly and evaluate the opinions of others without fear.

I am also more relaxed now. I no longer worry all the time about dying. Dad has even taught me how to goof off.

Not only do I enjoy being with Americans, I also enjoy being with Vietnamese. Living for fourteen years in Vietnam taught me many customs, subtleties and experiences. I like to talk with Vietnamese friends about "the good old times," the common activities, the famous places, and the popular food. What better joy is there than when you mention an episode in a less well-known novel and your friend recognizes it? This is like walking down the street in a foreign country and running into a friend from your home town. I also appreciate many Vietnamese customs like reverence and respect for the elderly, and the love and attention paid to small babies. In Vietnam, we never send older people to nursing homes or fail to pick up a crying baby.

There is a tension in being part of two families and two cultures. If the rest of my family comes to America, they too will have to pay a price. They will be happy to be reunited with the rest of us. They will no longer have to worry about what they will eat the next day. But they will miss the beauty and friendliness of Vietnam. They will miss the rain, the familiar sights in the market, the Tet celebrations that mark each year, the company of other shopkeepers.

I feel this tension even at school. Although I enjoy being with both Americans and Vietnamese, I often have to choose between them. At the University of Virginia cafeteria, the Vietnamese sit at one table, and Americans at others. If I sit with Vietnamese, American friends may question why I did not sit with them. If I sit with Americans, Vietnamese friends may question why I sit with people different than I. I have to choose and my choice may become a statement of something larger than it is intended to be.

For example, a few weeks ago when I entered the school cafeteria, I saw a Vietnamese friend sitting by himself at one table, and at the next table was an American girl who was also my friend. I concluded they did not know each other. I nodded to each, and because I wanted to sit with both of them, I asked the Vietnamese friend to join me in sitting with my American friend. To my surprise, he said he had almost finished eating and preferred to sit by himself.

I did not know what to do. Then I remembered the rule. Women first. I was relieved to find a principle on which to make my decision. As I sat down, I laughed because I realized that this was only one of the many difficult decisions I have made and will continue to make as a Vietnamese living in America.

As for my American family, we are more together than ever before. Mom and Dad have a good track record. They kept their commitment to us even when they learned that Ma and Ba were still alive. When I left for college Dad told me to call home any time day or night if I had a problem. If he could not solve the problem by telephone, he would come right away. I know that I can always go home when I need to, and that Mom and Dad will be there if I am in trouble. This gives me more support for going to college and doing other things on my own.

Finally, I am very proud of the young man my brother Nhi has become. We attend two different colleges. It is exciting to write letters and talk long distance on the telephone. We look forward to vacations when we can be together again. Before I felt a loss that he no longer needed me, but now I am proud to know that my brother is so independent. Our relationship is no longer one of desperate need, but true equality and brotherhood.

Epilogue
STEVE

During my first five years of marriage, I never imagined that I would become a father to two Vietnamese refugee boys. I always thought my children would be "home-made." Perhaps it was this notion of a more traditional family that was the reason I agonized so much over the decision to become a father to Nhi and Hy.

In retrospect, I am amazed that the decision seemed so difficult to me. God's call was as simple and clear as I have ever heard it: provide a home for these boys. On one level it seems that God's call is always unambiguous. Feed the hungry. Clothe the naked. Comfort the disheartened. Perhaps it was only my lack of faith that made complications in this matter—How will we provide for these boys? Where will we live? Am I even old enough to be a father to them?

My reservations proved totally unfounded. Through all our difficulties, Nhi and Hy have been a joy and a delight. Although I know we are not always rewarded on earth for our actions, it seems to me that this is one case in which we have truly been blessed a hundredfold.

Becoming a mother and father to Nhi and Hy has broadened substantially our view of family relationships. Now Debi and I worry less about "family planning." We fear that by focusing on our own desires we may not hear God's call to ministry, whatever that may be. Perhaps that ministry will include "children of our own," to borrow an awkward expression used to refer to God's children that we had a part in creating. Perhaps it will be a call to care for more of God's homeless children.

The needs of the world are so great and the number of

homeless children in America and around the world is so enormous that I have difficulty believing God will call us to create more children. A recent newspaper article spoke of "half a million minors, abandoned orphans, or roving delinquents" in Central America. Even as I write this, there are tens of thousands of refugees in Thailand as a result of the continuing war in surrounding countries. In Africa, Asia, Latin America, and in our own country, there are uncountable little ones who desperately need someone to call "Mom and Dad." Many of these, like Nhi, will suffer devastating physical blows for lack of proper medical care. (Nhi would be walking today had the war not prevented him from receiving a polio vaccine that costs only a few cents.)

In the meantime, Debi and I try to keep open hearts and prayerful spirits. If someday soon we hear a call similar to the one that brought Nhi and Hy into our lives, we trust that we will be able to answer, "Here am I, Lord, send me."

Acknowledgments

Our special thanks go to two friends who made this book possible. Barbara Thompson, a gifted writer, helped us turn a collection of family stories into an integrated whole. Her laughter and work lifted us over many hurdles during an unforgettable month in her rustic North Carolina cabin. Roxanna Johnson selflessly spent long hours editing and typing. Her suggestions, enthusiasm, and stamina gave life to our book.

Four people offered unique inspiration as our book progressed:
—Mr. Vuong Hung Nguyen, a former Saigon staff member for *Newsweek* and *The New Yorker,* helped us bridge many gaps between East and West as he explained Vietnamese culture, history, and people. Our book would have been richer if he had lived to see its completion; we mourn his untimely death and that he could not see the book in final form.
—Linda Hudak, now a Yale Medical student preparing to serve low income Americans, read our first few tentative drafts before we had the courage to tell anyone else what we were writing. She compared her own experiences from teaching Laotian refugees in Ubon, Thailand, and shared her vision for what the book could become.
—Connie Nash, who adopted two older Ugandan boys, lent insight gained from her own joys and struggles in forming a new family.
—Diana Shaw, an accomplished writer living on the West Coast, greatly encouraged us in our first effort.

Four friends patiently proofread the final copy: Chris Burman, who teaches refugee parents how to help their children succeed in school; Florence Frey, who first met Nhi and Hy while working with Debi and Steve in Songkhla Refugee Camp; Julie Hamre, a lay leader at Luther Place Church in caring for refugees and the homeless; and Betty Woodruff, President of Hannah House shelter for homeless women. Betty also let us use her lakeside

West Virginia cottage, where we completed the manuscript in peace and beauty.

We are grateful to Al Bryant, our editor, and all the helpful people at Word Books. We also want to thank our agent, Hershel Shanks, and our photographer, Mimi Levine.

Our story grew out of an incredible, vibrant church, started forty years ago by Gordon Cosby, his wife Mary, and her sister Elizabeth-Anne Campagna. In 1979, Robert Bainum planted the seeds for COSIGN, Church of the Saviour's mission group that made it possible for hundreds of people to work in the refugee camps. Jerry Aitken and Chet Jamavan provided continuity and supervision in the camps while Helen Cary, Elizabeth O'Connor, and many others organized and prayed for the flow of volunteers.

And finally, we are grateful to everyone who loved and supported us while the four of us grew together as a family.